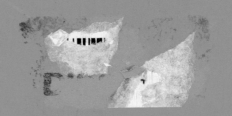

AFR 03

PLEASE DO NOT REMOVE
CARD FROM POCKET

1 booklet of lyrics in pocket

A READER'S DIGEST SONGBOOK

REMEMBERING YESTERDAY'S HITS

Editor: William L. Simon
Music arranged and edited by Dan Fox
Project Editor: Mary Kelleher
Associate Editor: Natalie Moreda
Designer: Karen Mastropietro
Music Associate: Elizabeth Mead

Annotated by Jim Lowe

READER'S DIGEST GENERAL BOOKS
Editorial Director: John A. Pope, Jr.
Managing Editor: Jane Polley
Art Director: Richard J. Berenson
Group Editors: Norman B. Mack, John Speicher,
David Trooper (Art), Susan J. Wernert

THE READER'S DIGEST ASSOCIATION, INC.
Pleasantville, New York/Montreal

ISBN 0-89577-249-3

Printed in the United States of America

INDEX TO SECTIONS

INDEX TO SONGS

*Instrumental

2

Introduction

Calling all nostalgia lovers, trivia buffs and, of course, music fans of all stripes — have we got a book for you! Think back to those happy bygone days of Your Hit Parade, the immensely popular radio and, later, television program that each week from 1935 to 1957 documented America's top song hits. No fewer than 50 (count 'em, 50) of the 91 songs in this book attained the coveted No. 1 position on the show. Of the remainder, some reached the runner-up spot, some were No. 1 best-selling records, and some were best-sellers before charts became the music industry's yardstick of popularity.

As always, the musical arrangements were specially commissioned by us. And, once again, they're by Dan Fox. Dan has arranged all of our songbooks, beginning with the first one, which we published in 1969. Over the years, he has delighted us — and, we hope, you — with brand-new arrangements for more than 1,000 songs, both old and new.

And, as with our previous books, the repertoire of this one was compiled by Bill Simon, musician and musicologist. Bill, who was Senior Music Editor of the Digest's Recorded Music Division for many years, continues to be in charge of our songbook program.

We'd also like to introduce — for those who don't know him already — a new addition to our songbook team, radio personality and pop-music maven Jim Lowe. If reading the "stories behind the songs" that Jim has written for us reawakens some of your happiest memories, well, that's the general idea. It's the sort of happy occurrence that takes place daily on New York City's "good music" radio station, WNEW, where Jim — the acclaimed King of Trivia — presides. Jim takes to the music business naturally. He spent much of his childhood in his grandfather's music store in Springfield, Missouri, and learned about Bing Crosby, Ruth Etting and The Mills Brothers long before he found out that Franklin D. Roosevelt was President of the United States. Later, he got to know about song hits firsthand. In 1953, he wrote "Gambler's Guitar," which sold a million records for Rusty Draper. And three years later, his own recording of "The Green Door" sold 2 million copies. Most of the artists and songwriters Jim discusses on these pages became his personal friends.

As is obvious from our 11 music books — with more to come in the future — the reservoir of great popular songs is bottomless. But not every hit song is suitable for parlor pianists. Most contemporary hits, for example, rely more on recording techniques than on melody, harmony or lyrics. It's impossible to duplicate such effects on your own piano, organ or guitar. But we hope that the younger musicians in your home will discover and share with you and us the many joys that were built into "our" songs back in the 1920s, '30s, '40s and '50s.

Working on this collection of yesterday's hits has been a joy. We trust that it will give you as much pleasure as putting it together gave us.

HOW TO USE THIS SONGBOOK

The arrangements in this book were designed to be easy to play while still being musically interesting and artistically gratifying. For players of any treble clef instrument, the melody is on top, clear and uncluttered, with the stems of the notes turned up. However, if one is to play in tandem with a piano or organ, it must be on a "C" instrument, such as a violin, flute, recorder, oboe, accordion, harmonica, melodica or any of the new electronic keyboards. Guitarists can also play the melody as written, or they can play chords from the symbols (G7, Am, etc.) or from the diagrams printed just above the staves. Organists whose instruments have foot pedals may use the small *pedal notes* in the bass clef (with stems turned down). But these pedal notes should not be attempted by pianists; *they are for feet only!* For the sake of facility, the pedal lines move stepwise and stay within an octave. Players who improvise in the jazz sense can "take off" from the melody and the chord symbols.

The chord symbols also are designed for pianists who have studied the popular chord method; players can read the melody line and improvise their own left-hand accompaniments. The chord symbols may be used, too, by bass players (string or brass); just play the root note of each chord symbol, except where another note is indicated (for example, "D/F# bass"). Accordionists can use the chord symbols for the left-hand buttons while playing the treble portions of the arrangement as written.

—The Editors

Section 1
HITS FROM THE SHOWS

from *On a Clear Day You Can See Forever*

Words by Alan Jay Lerner; Music by Burton Lane

ON A CLEAR DAY
(You Can See Forever)

On a Clear Day You Can See Forever opened on Broadway in 1965 to mixed reviews. The plot of the musical, by its lyricist, Alan Jay Lerner, revolves around reincarnation and extrasensory perception. (Under hypnosis by a psychiatrist in order to stop smoking, a girl decides that she has lived an earlier life, in 19th-century England.) Lerner had just had a phenomenally successful decade, what with My Fair Lady *and* Camelot, *both written with Frederick Loewe. For* On a Clear Day, *his collaborator was the veteran composer Burton Lane (Finian's Rainbow; Royal Wedding). Barbara Harris starred as the ESP conduit on Broadway; Barbra Streisand played the role in the film version. The title song was sung on stage by John Cullum as the psychiatrist and in the film by Yves Montand. It later became a hit recording by Robert Goulet. Although addressing the theme of the show directly, it has the feel of a love ballad. It is traditional in its AABA construction, but the elevation of the second eight bars gives it an airy, soaring feeling, lifting it above the banal.*

On a Clear Day (You Can See Forever)

HEART

from *Damn Yankees*

Words and Music by Richard Adler and Jerry Ross

"Heart" and the next two songs in this book have a common — and tragic — denominator. They come from the only two Broadway musicals written by the team of Richard Adler and Jerry Ross. The partnership was severed by Ross's death at the much too early age of 29. "Heart" is from Damn Yankees, based on Douglass Wallop's novel The Year the Yankees Lost the Pennant. The 1955 Faustian show starred Gwen Verdon as the witch Lola, who tempts a baseball fan to sell his soul to the Devil (Ray Walston) in exchange for a chance to play for the Washington Senators. (And, as another hit from the show put it, whatever Lola wanted, Lola got.) Largely through Eddie Fisher's recording, "Heart" became one of the big hits of the year, vying for position in the Top Ten with "Hernando's Hideaway" from Adler and Ross's The Pajama Game.

Moderate soft-shoe tempo

You've got-ta have heart; All you real-ly need is heart. When the odds are say-in' you'll nev-er win,— That's when the grin— should start. You've got-ta have

HEY THERE

from *The Pajama Game* **Words and Music by Richard Adler and Jerry Ross**

"Hey There" first saw the light of day in Richard Adler and Jerry Ross's 1954 hit musical The Pajama Game, *which was based on Richard Bissell's novel* 7½ Cents. *The original cast version was sung by John Raitt, in the role of the superintendent of a pajama factory. If you remember that he sang it into a dictaphone, give yourself 7½ trivia points. Through the 1950s and well into the '60s, whenever Columbia or RCA Victor recorded the cast album of a show, you could bet that at least one of their top singers would soon record at least one song from it. In the case of* The Pajama Game, *the company was Columbia, the song was "Hey There" and the performer was Rosemary Clooney, then one of the hottest wax artists in the country. "Hey There" was a No. 1 hit for Rosemary in the late summer of 1954, and also became a successful recording for Sammy Davis, Jr.*

Hey There

HERNANDO'S HIDEAWAY

from *The Pajama Game*

Words and Music by Richard Adler and Jerry Ross

Through most of the 1950s, Arthur Godfrey was the king of network television and radio. His musical conductor at that time was Archie Bleyer, whom Godfrey fired, along with singer Julius La Rosa. Bleyer's misdemeanor was to have started his own record company, Cadence, which, in time, became very successful. One of the label's biggest hits was Archie's own recording of "Hernando's Hideaway." Richard Adler and Jerry Ross used the song in The Pajama Game *as an elaborate spoof of the tango. Keeping the Latin tempo intact, Archie's vocal group's quiet staccato approach gave the words just the right touch. Also, the recording, it should be noted, gave castanets a good name. The song reached No. 1 on* Your Hit Parade *and remained on the survey for 14 weeks in 1954.*

13

BUT NOT FOR ME

from *Girl Crazy*   Words by Ira Gershwin; Music by George Gershwin

Ginger Rogers

In "But Not for Me," we find lyricist Ira Gershwin in his best form, with lines like "With love to lead the way, I've found more clouds of gray than any Russian play could guarantee" and, as the denouement, "When ev'ry happy plot ends with the marriage knot, and there's no knot for me." The song is from the explosive 1930 musical Girl Crazy, which made a star of a lady who would go on to become the leading performer of the Great White Way. But Ethel Merman didn't sing this song in the show. Rather, it was warbled by a young lady who arrived in New York by way of Texas and Missouri. Her name was Ginger Rogers, and she became, of course, better known for her dancing and beauty than for her singing. But her ingratiating vocal style allowed her to put "But Not for Me" across handsomely. Verses aren't often sung these days, but this one is so special that we had to include it, if for no other reason than that Gershwin rhymed "try it" and "riot."

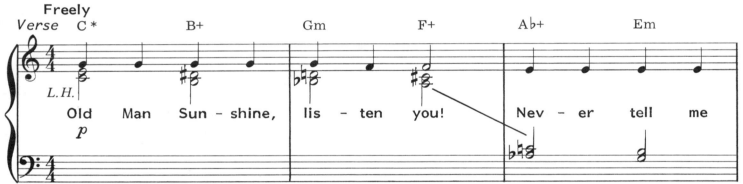

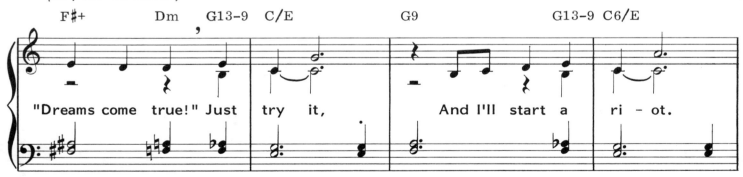

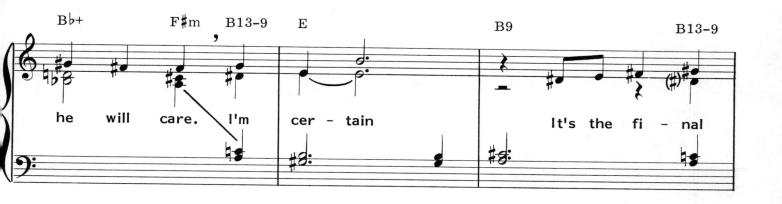

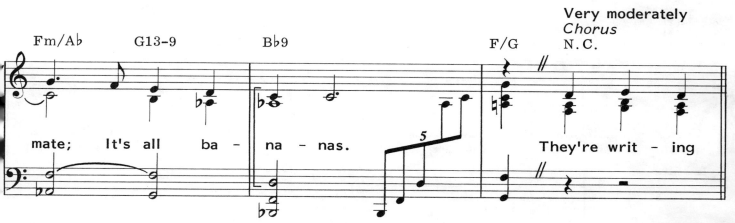

* on verse, chord symbols are for keyboard only. Guitar, if used, comes in at the chorus.
** the "Ann Landers" or "Dear Abby" of her day

But Not for Me

Since they're probably the three most popular words in the English language, it was inevitable that "I Love You" should serve as the title of more than one song. One was from a 1923 Broadway musical called Little Jessie James. Another served as the theme song for a band led by Tommy Tucker. But the best of all possible "I Love You"s comes from a 1944 Cole Porter musical called Mexican Hayride. And yet, when the show opened at the Winter Garden Theatre, critics were lukewarm about the score. Porter — as if he had to — would answer later with the hit-laden Kiss Me Kate and his excellent songs for the film High Society. But even had he never written another lyric, "It's spring again, / And birds on the wing again / Start to sing again / The old melody" should have been proof positive that his musical well was far from dry.

from *Mexican Hayride*

Words and Music by Cole Porter

I Love You

Bewitched

The 1940 Rodgers and Hart Broadway classic Pal Joey was based on a hard-hitting story by John O'Hara and was the first musical in which a heel (Gene Kelly) was the protagonist. It's also often cited as the first musical in which the songs were integrated into the plot — although there had been flashes of this in other shows, as early as Show Boat in 1927. But in earlier years, when creating musicals, most songwriters simply delved deep into their "trunks" and pulled out tunes that had been written and placed on hold, as it were, until they could be interpolated into a show. Besides "I Could Write a Book," "You Mustn't Kick It Around" and other songs, Pal Joey produced "Bewitched," sung by the aging female lead, who is in love with the young Joey and in the song addresses the pitfalls of a May-December romance.

from *Pal Joey*
Words by Lorenz Hart
Music by Richard Rodgers

Slowly, in 2 (♩=1 beat)

Verse

He's a fool and don't I know it, But a fool can have his charms.
Love's the same old sad sen-sa-tion; Late-ly I've not slept a wink,

I'm in love and don't I show it, Since this half-pint im-i-ta-tion

1. Like a babe in arms?

2. Put me on the blink. I'm

Bewitched

It's De-Lovely

Ethel Merman

Jimmy Durante

from *Red, Hot and Blue!*
Words and Music by Cole Porter

The year was 1936. Ethel Merman and Jimmy Durante were big Broadway names, few bigger. For the musical Red, Hot and Blue!, *they were joined by a young comedian whose fame in time would eclipse theirs. Bob Hope would, in fact, dominate America's funny men for decades to come. But* Red, Hot and Blue! *was Merman's show. In addition to "It's De-Lovely" (which she sang with Hope), she also introduced "Ridin' High" and "Down in the Depths, on the Ninetieth Floor." For Cole Porter, who wrote the score for the show, with a libretto by the noted playwriting team of Howard Lindsay and Russell Crouse, 1936 was a busy and productive year. One of the first of the bi-coastal tunesmiths, Porter also scored heavily that year in Hollywood with the tunes for his first film assignment, MGM's* Born to Dance, *which included "Easy to Love" and "I've Got You Under My Skin." Not bad for a fellow who a decade before had been dismissed as a dilettante, simply because he had gone to Yale, was a millionaire in his own right, had lived the sophisticated life of a wealthy expatriate in Paris and Venice before moving to New York, and had probably never even seen the Lower East Side, that spawning ground for so many of America's great popular songwriters.*

*pronounced "de-lukes"

from *Wish You Were Here*
Words and Music by Harold Rome

WISH YOU WERE HERE

Eddie Fisher

There's a common denominator between the 1952 musical Wish You Were Here and singer Eddie Fisher, who turned this title song from the show into a best-selling recording. Fisher got his start as a performer in the Catskill Mountains of New York State, and that is the mise-en-scène of the show. As noted earlier, when the record companies, particularly the two largest, RCA and Columbia, did a cast album, they saw to it that their biggest artists also recorded the best songs from the show. (Sometimes they had a financial interest in the show themselves, as was the case with Columbia and My Fair Lady.) For "Wish You Were Here," RCA chose Eddie Fisher, at that time in the Army but still turning out hit after hit for the label. (Jack Cassidy sang the song on Broadway.) Wish You Were Here, with its score by Harold Rome and under the direction of Joshua Logan, will always be remembered as having had a swimming pool on the stage. It will also always be remembered for this lovely song.

Moderate Latin feel (in 2, each ♩ = 1 beat)

They're not mak-ing the skies as blue this year. Wish you were here! As blue as they used to when you were near. Wish you were here! And the

Wish You Were Here

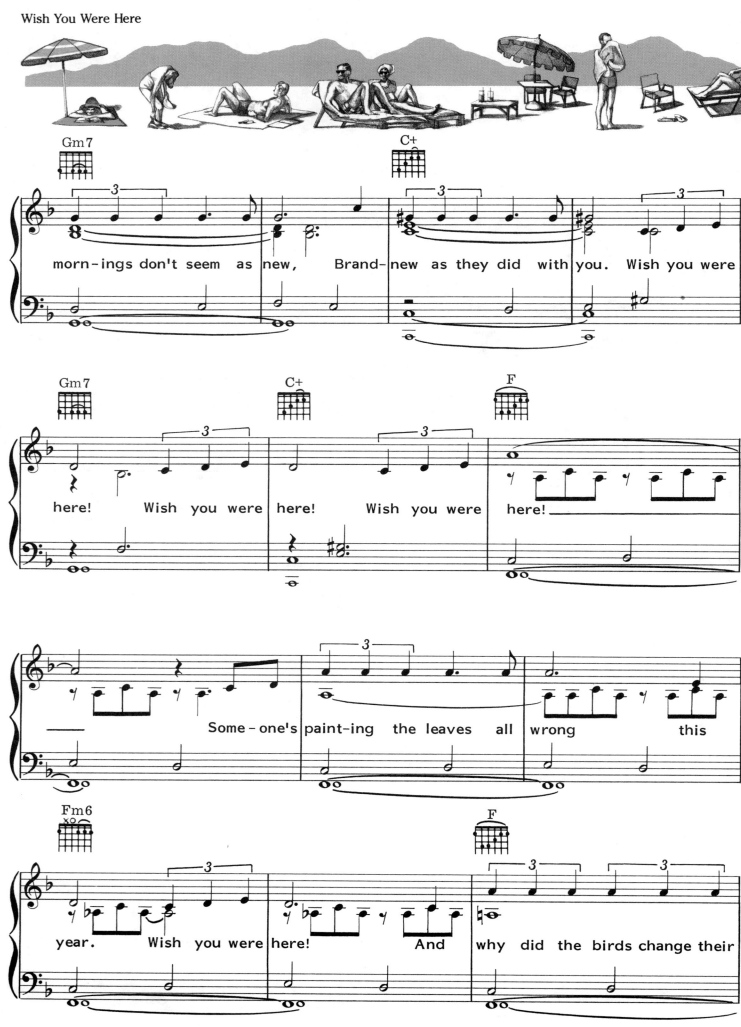

morn-ings don't seem as new, Brand-new as they did with you. Wish you were

here! Wish you were here! Wish you were here!_____

_____ Some-one's paint-ing the leaves all wrong this

year. Wish you were here! And why did the birds change their

Where or When

from
Babes in Arms

Words by Lorenz Hart; Music by Richard Rodgers

"Where or When," from the 1937 Babes in Arms, *appeared on* Your Hit Parade *for almost the entire summer of that year. The first song to address the subject of déjà vu, it shows Lorenz Hart at his remarkable best ("The clothes you're wearing are the clothes you wore"; "Some things that happen for the first time seem to be happening again"), accompanied by one of Richard Rodgers' most celebrated melodies.* Babes in Arms *contained one of the composing team's strongest scores, perhaps the strongest of all as far as songs that have become standards are concerned. In addition to "Where or When," the show offered "The Lady Is a Tramp," "I Wish I Were in Love Again," "My Funny Valentine" and "Johnny One Note."*

Last 3 bars may be sung an 8va lower.

Yesterdays

from *Roberta*

Words by Otto Harbach; Music by Jerome Kern

"Yesterdays" is one of the most poignant and appealing of all of Jerome Kern's songs, and the lovely melody — like so many of Kern's, rangy and somewhat unpredictable — is matched by Otto Harbach's sensitive, nostalgic lyric. It's from Roberta (1933) and was sung as the lady of the title, an aging couturière, lay dying. The Broadway cast included a bumper crop of future Hollywood greats, among them Bob Hope, Fred MacMur-

ray, George Murphy and a rotund British import who became one of filmdom's favorite heavies, Sidney Greenstreet. Besides "Yesterdays," the milestone score included the immortal "Smoke Gets in Your Eyes," "The Touch of Your Hand" and "You're Devastating." Roberta soon found its way to Tinsel Town and became a vehicle for Fred Astaire and Ginger Rogers, along with Irene Dunne and Randolph Scott.

Slowly, but without dragging

They Didn't Believe Me

There is a growing conviction that if a listing were made of the top 100 songwriters in the history of Broadway and Hollywood, Jerome Kern would emerge as No. 1. He was the master of melody, creating big, sweeping, majestic songs that transcend time and point of origin. For proof, examine "They Didn't Believe Me," written, unbelievably, in 1914! It doesn't have the scope of some of his later ballads, but it is beautifully constructed, and the notes that accompany the title itself somehow fit it just perfectly. The song was one of seven tunes that Kern wrote for an

Words by Herbert Reynolds; Music by Jerome Kern

Jerome Kern

English musical called **The Girl from Utah.** *All were interpolated into the show when it came to New York. (The plot revolves around — what else? — a girl from Utah who, trying to avoid a polygamous marriage to a Mormon, flees her native state and goes to London.) Beginning with the film version of* Roberta, *for which he added "I Won't Dance" and "Lovely to Look At" for Fred Astaire and Ginger Rogers, Kern spent nearly all of the last decade of his life in Hollywood, writing such song classics as "The Way You Look Tonight," "I'm Old Fashioned" and "Long Ago (and Far Away)."*

They Didn't Believe Me

Your lips, your eyes, your cheeks, your hair Are in a class be-yond com-
Your lips, your eyes, your curl - y hair Are in a class be-yond com-

pare; You're the love-li-est girl That one could see!
pare; You're the love-li-est thing That one could see!

And when I tell them, And I cert-'nly am goin' to tell them,
And when I tell them, And I cert-'nly am goin' to tell them,

That I'm the man whose wife one day you'll be,
That I'm the girl whose boy one day you'll be,

NO OTHER LOVE

from *Me and Juliet*

Words by Oscar Hammerstein II; Music by Richard Rodgers

By the time Richard Rodgers and Oscar Hammerstein II wrote Me and Juliet *in 1953, they had already established themselves as the most successful team in the history of the musical theater. Such dazzling smashes as* Oklahoma!, Carousel, South Pacific *and* The King and I *had all appeared on Broadway (the last two were still running in 1953), and they had all been produced in a period of less than 10 years! With such triumphs, it's hard to believe that people weren't standing in line for all of their shows, but even Rodgers and Hammerstein didn't top themselves every time out. However, even their secondary shows, such as* Flower Drum Song *and* Me and Juliet, *would have been considered successes by most songwriters' criteria. The latter musical ran for 358 performances and, thanks largely to Perry Como's recording, produced this popular song hit. Actually, Rodgers had used the melody before. It was first heard as "Beneath the Southern Cross," one of the themes from his score for the television series* Victory at Sea.

Perry Como

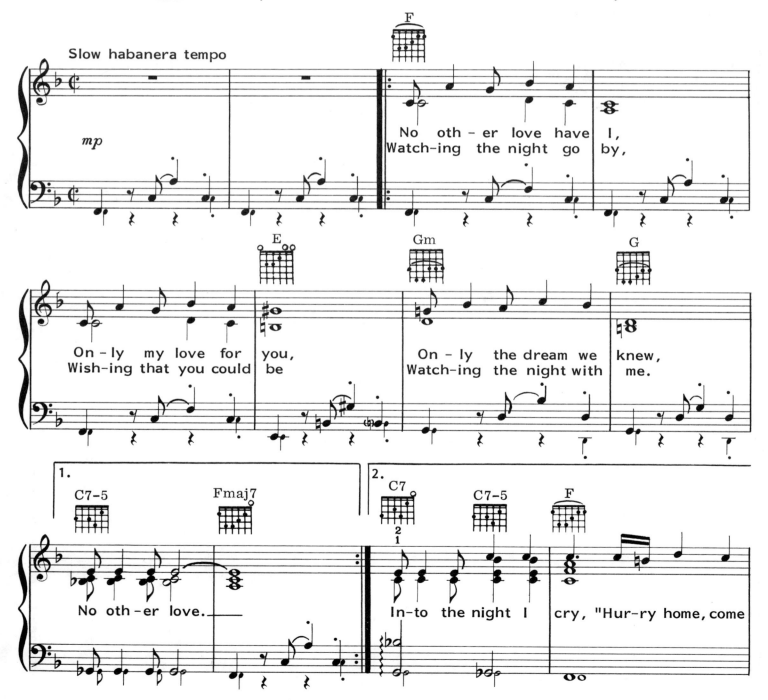

Slow habanera tempo

No oth-er love have I,
Watch-ing the night go by,

On-ly my love for you,
Wish-ing that you could be

On-ly the dream we knew,
Watch-ing the night with me.

1.
No oth-er love.

2.
In-to the night I cry, "Hur-ry home, come

40

from *Cats*

From words by Trevor Nunn after T.S. Eliot; Music by Andrew Lloyd Webber

Andrew Lloyd Webber, whose previous successes include Evita, Joseph and the Amazing Technicolor Dreamcoat *and* Jesus Christ, Superstar, *produced one of the greatest musical hits in history with* Cats, *which opened on Broadway in 1982. Based on T.S. Eliot's book of poems* Old Possum's Book of Practical Cats, *the show is a feline fancier's fantasy, filled with the antics of Gumbiecat, Rum Tum Tugger, Old Deuteronomy, Mungojerrie and others. A famous song-writer is alleged to have remarked that every song should be a little familiar. With "Memory," the hit song from* Cats, *sung by Grizabella the Glamour Cat, Webber may have overdone it; guesses as to the melody's musical origins run from Ravel to Offenbach and Puccini. The interesting lyric, which* Cats *director Trevor Nunn adapted from Eliot's poetry, takes up from "Midnight, not a sound from the pavement" to "The stale cold smell of morning" and "A new day has begun." These words should keep singers purring for a long time.*

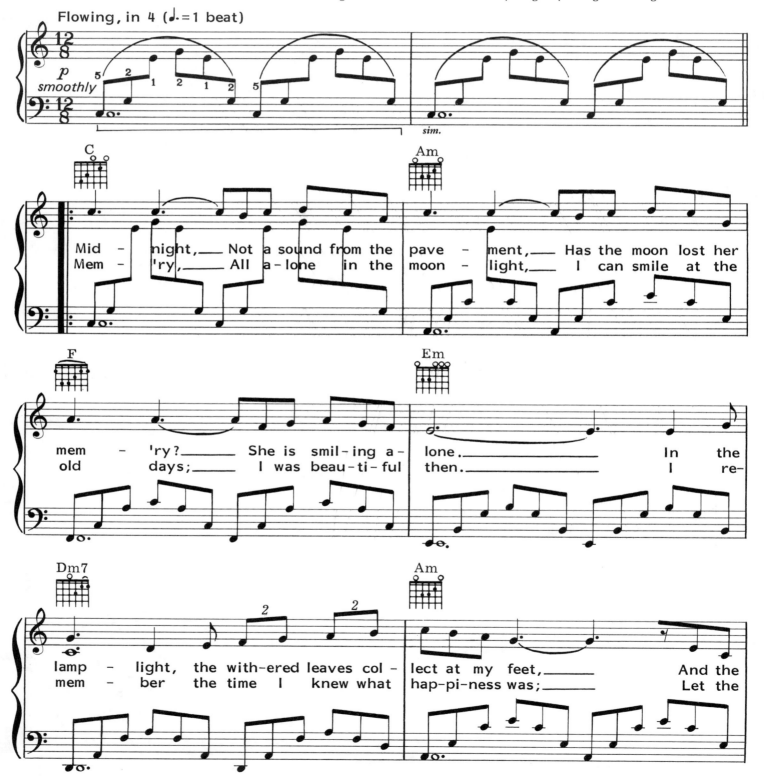

42

Section 2
HITS FROM HOLLYWOOD FILMS

Words by Johnny Mercer
Music by Jerome Kern

from *You Were Never Lovelier*

I'm Old Fashioned

"I'm Old Fashioned" was introduced in the 1942 Columbia musical You Were Never Lovelier, *which starred Fred Astaire, Rita Hayworth (it was their second film together; their first,* You'll Never Get Rich, *had appeared the year before), Adolphe Menjou and Xavier Cugat. The movie marked the first collaboration between Jerome Kern and Johnny Mercer and produced three exquisite ballads — the title tune, "Dearly Beloved" and this song, which is made up of one of Kern's loveliest melodies and one of Mercer's favorites among all the lyrics he wrote. Even today, the film — despite its rather silly mistaken-identity plot — holds up well, thanks to the beauty and power of these songs and the beautiful dancing they inspired. Unfortunately, Kern and Mercer collaborated only once more (on "Two Hearts Are Better Than One" for the film* Centennial Summer) *before Kern's death in 1945. However, with "I'm Old Fashioned" alone, they left a great legacy.*

With a lilt

mp

F   Gm11   C7   Fmaj7   Gm11   C7

I'm   old   fash-ioned;   I   love   the   moon - light;   I

I'm Old Fashioned

*Pianists: Release C to play these 2 measures.

from Exodus
Words by Pat Boone; Music by Ernest Gold

THE EXODUS SONG

Composer Ernest Gold's "Exodus" was the title theme for Otto Preminger's 1960 blockbuster film. It was used as a recurring motif throughout the movie, which concerned the modern immigration of Jews into Palestine before the state of Israel was established. With Exodus, Gold won an Academy Award for Outstanding Score of a Dramatic Film and also received a Grammy from the National Academy of Recording Arts and Sciences for Song of the Year. The theme became a best-selling instrumental recording via a two-piano rendition by the team of Ferrante & Teicher which was on the charts for five months and reached No. 2 in the Top Ten in the spring of 1961. Singer Pat Boone later wrote the lyrics for Gold's melody that are included here and recorded his version of the song under the title "The Exodus Song (This Land Is Mine)."

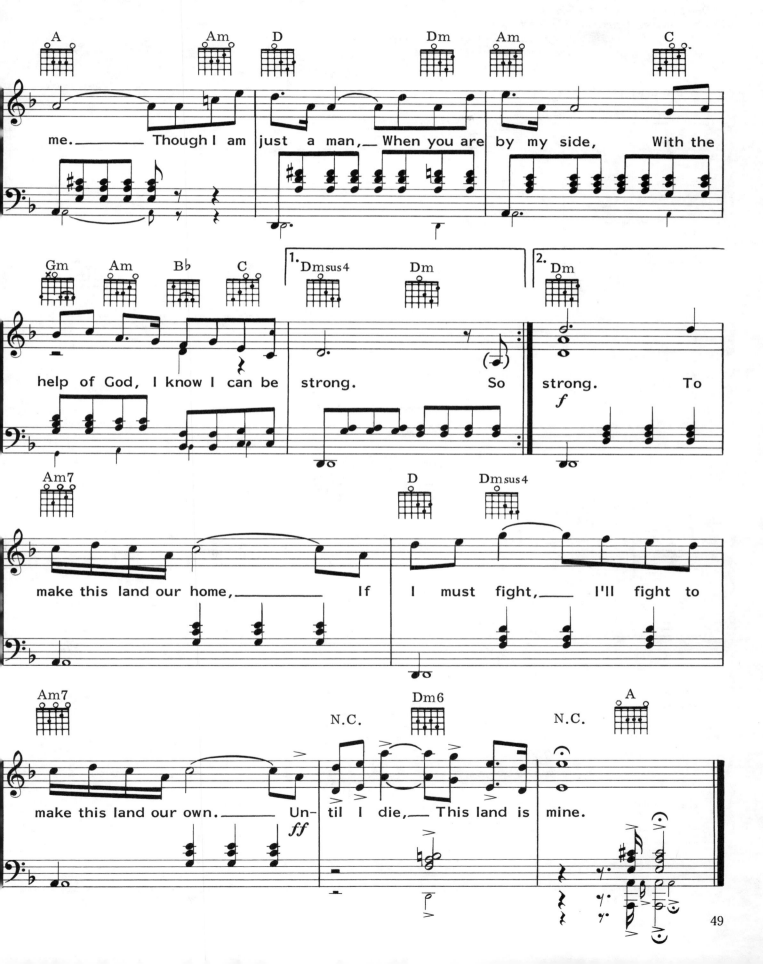

I'LL GET BY
(As Long As I Have You)

from *A Guy Named Joe*

Words by
Roy Turk;
Music by
Fred E. Ahlert

"I'll Get By," written in 1928, was one of the biggest hits of the late '20s and became a hit again in 1943 when it served as the theme of the Spencer Tracy-Irene Dunne film A Guy Named Joe. *Roy Turk and Fred Ahlert collaborated on a number of other standards, including "Mean to Me," "I Don't Know Why," "Walkin' My Baby Back Home" and Bing Crosby's theme, "Where the Blue of the Night (Meets the Gold of the Day)." Besides being a composer of no small merit, Ahlert worked for many years for the music-licensing organization known as ASCAP, first as a director and later as president.*

Slow and rhythmic

mp nice and easy

I'll get by ___ As long as I ___ Have you. ___ Though there be rain ___ And dark-ness too, ___ I'll not com - plain, ___ I'll

Love Walked In

from *The Goldwyn Follies*

Words by Ira Gershwin; Music by George Gershwin

"Love Walked In" was introduced in The Goldwyn Follies, *a 1938 musical that starred Adolphe Menjou, Andrea Leeds, Vera Zorina and The Ritz Brothers. The film, a rather mediocre hodgepodge revolving around a frantic producer (Menjou) who hires Miss Leeds to judge his movies from the average filmgoer's point of view, contains several of George Gershwin's last songs — "Love Is Here to Stay," "I Was Doing All Right" and this lovely tune, which Gershwin referred to as his "Brahmsian" melody. The composer died while writing the score, which was completed by Vernon Duke. In the last year of his*

life, Gershwin produced a string of standards that is virtually unmatched in American popular songwriting — "Shall We Dance?," "They All Laughed," "They Can't Take That Away from Me," "Let's Call the Whole Thing Off," "Things Are Looking Up," "A Foggy Day" and "Nice Work If You Can Get It," besides the three Goldwyn Follies songs. The fact that he had to audition for Sam Goldwyn provides an interesting example of the low esteem that Hollywood had for songwriters in the '30s. But as George's lyricist brother Ira asked in their song "They All Laughed": "Who's got the last laugh now?"

I Can't Begin to Tell You

from *The Dolly Sisters*

Words by Mack Gordon
Music by James V. Monaco

Betty Grable

Betty Grable introduced "I Can't Begin to Tell You" in the 1945 20th Century-Fox musical The Dolly Sisters. This was among the last songs written by composer James V. Monaco, whose career stretched back to 1912, when he first caught the public's imagination with his melodies "You Made Me Love You" and "Row, Row, Row." In 1927, in the first "talking" film, The Jazz Singer, Al Jolson sang "Dirty Hands, Dirty Face" — by none other than Jimmy Monaco. The songwriter went to Hollywood in 1930 and contributed tunes to more of the early "talkies." He also had his own dance orchestra in the mid-'30s. Then, in 1936, he went to work at Paramount Studios, where, along with Johnny Burke, he wrote for no fewer than seven Bing Crosby films. Among his best-known songs of this period were "On the Sentimental Side," "I've Got a Pocketful of Dreams," "An Apple for the Teacher" and "Only Forever." When his partnership with Burke ended, Monaco wrote with several other lyricists, receiving Academy Award nominations for "We Mustn't Say Goodbye" (1943), "I'm Making Believe" (1944) and, with Mack Gordon, "I Can't Begin to Tell You," which hit the top of Your Hit Parade in 1945, the year he died at the age of 60.

Slowly

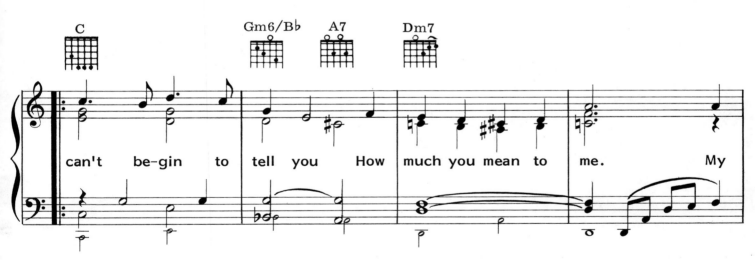

can't be-gin to tell you How much you mean to me. My

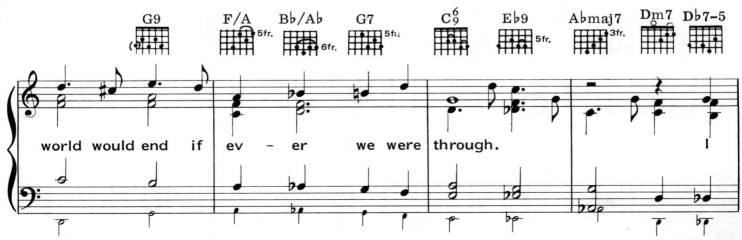

world would end if ev – er we were through.

All Through the Day

from *Centennial Summer*

Words by Oscar Hammerstein II; Music by Jerome Kern

This song was written for the 1946 20th Century-Fox musical Centennial Summer, *which was set during the Philadelphia Exposition of 1876 and involved sisters Jeanne Crain and Linda Darnell pursuing Cornel Wilde. The real riches of the movie lie in the exquisite score — his last complete*

one — by composer Jerome Kern. In the process, Kern worked with three lyricists — Johnny Mercer ("Two Hearts Are Better Than One"), Leo Robin ("In Love in Vain") and Oscar Hammerstein II ("All Through the Day"). Kern and Hammerstein had collaborated often in the past, creating such shows as Show Boat ("Can't Help Lovin' Dat Man," "Ol' Man River," "Only Make Believe," "Why Do I Love You?"), Very Warm for May ("All the Things You Are") and Music in the Air ("I've Told Ev'ry Little Star"). Kern died in 1945, before Centennial Summer was released, after a heart attack in New York City at the age of 60.

Ac-cent-tchu-ate the Positive
(Mister In-Between)

from *Here Come the Waves*

Words by Johnny Mercer; Music by Harold Arlen

Bing Crosby introduced "Ac-cent-tchu-ate the Positive" in Here Come the Waves, *a 1944 Paramount musical in which Bing co-starred with Betty Hutton. The song featured music by*

Bing Crosby

Harold Arlen and lyrics by Johnny Mercer. These inspired collaborators had already received Academy Award nominations for "Blues in the Night" (1941), "That Old Black Magic" (1942) and "My Shining Hour" (1943). They were nominated for the fourth time in four years with "Ac-cent-tchu-ate the Positive," losing to Johnny Burke and Jimmy Van Heusen's "Swinging on a Star," from another Crosby film, Going My Way. *On Broadway in 1946, Arlen and Mercer teamed up on* St. Louis Woman, *which was a commercial failure. But not many Broadway hits boast as impressive a score as this "flop." From it came "Come Rain or Come Shine," "Any Place I Hang My Hat Is Home," "Legalize My Name" and "A Woman's Prerogative."*

from *Gold Diggers of 1935*   **Words by Al Dubin; Music by Harry Warren**

"Lullaby of Broadway," introduced by Wini Shaw in Gold Diggers of 1935, *was the second song to receive an Academy Award (the first was "The Continental" from* The Gay Divorcee *the previous year). Among the many other famous songs that Al Dubin and Harry Warren composed before their nine-year partnership ended in 1939 were "Forty-Second Street," "Shuffle Off to Buffalo," "You're Getting to Be a Habit with Me," "The Boulevard of Broken Dreams," "I Only Have Eyes for You," "About a Quarter to Nine" and "September in the Rain." "Lullaby of Broadway" and other Warren-Dubin tunes were revived — with great success — in the long-running musical* Forty-Second Street, *which opened on Broadway in 1980.*

LULLABY OF BROADWAY

Light, bouncy swing

Come on a-long and lis-ten to___ The lull-a-by of Broad-way.
Come on a-long and lis-ten to___ The lull-a-by of Broad-way.

The hip hoo-ray and bal-ly-hoo,___ The lull-a-by of Broad-way.
The hi-dee-hi and boop-a-doo,___ The lull-a-by of Broad-way.

The rum-ble of a sub-way train,___ The rat-tle of the tax-is,
The band be-gins to go to town,___ And ev-'ry-one goes cra-zy.

I Couldn't

Words by Harold Adamson
Music by Jimmy McHugh

"I Couldn't Sleep a Wink Last Night" first appeared in the 1943 RKO musical Higher and Higher, *sung by a young man making his acting debut in films — Frank Sinatra. In the movie, Sinatra, who received third billing behind Michele Morgan and Jack Haley, also sang "The Music Stopped" and "A Lovely Way to Spend an Evening." For trivia buffs, this wasn't Sinatra's first film appearance. He had previously appeared as a singer in* Las Vegas Nights *(1941),* Ship Ahoy *(1942) and* Reveille with Beverly *(1943). Not long after, Sinatra moved on to greater Hollywood fame in a series of MGM musicals, including* Anchors Aweigh *and* On the Town. *If you should see* Higher and Higher *on late-night TV and watch carefully, you might catch a glimpse of another aspiring young singer — a teenaged Mel Tormé.*

Sleep a Wink Last Night

from Higher and Higher

from
Diamond Horseshoe

The More I See You

Words by Mack Gordon — Music by Harry Warren

Dick Haymes — Betty Grable

"The More I See You" is from the 1945 20th Century-Fox musical Diamond Horseshoe. *The film was set in showman-composer Billy Rose's famous New York City cabaret of that name and starred Dick Haymes as a stagestruck young doctor and Betty Grable as a gold-digging nightclub girl. By this time, Harry Warren and Mack Gordon's partnership was in full bloom. The two had received Academy Award* nominations for four consecutive years and were the top songwriting team at Fox. "The More I See You" is one of their loveliest tunes and has that rare quality of seeming to sing itself. Diamond Horseshoe, *which also featured the lovely "I Wish I Knew," was Warren's last chore for Fox. Soon after, he moved to MGM, where he wrote a series of outstanding scores, including the one for* The Harvey Girls.

Words by Johnny Burke
Music by Jimmy Van Heusen

from *Dixie*

Bing Crosby introduced "Sunday, Monday or Always" in the 1943 Paramount musical Dixie. (Bing also sang it off screen in The Road to Utopia two years later.) This was just about the time during World War II when Bing was evolving from a superstar into a world figure. Despite Bing's movie and No. 1 Decca Record versions, "Sunday, Monday or

Always" is also closely identified with Frank Sinatra. Sinatra cut the song (one of his initial solo efforts with Columbia) in June 1943, during the ban on all recording called by the musicians' union. Because of the ban, instead of an orchestra to supply the musical background on the record, a vocal chorus — the Bobby Tucker Singers — was substituted.

Bing Crosby

Sunday, Monday or Always

Slowly, with expression

Won't you tell me when
We will meet a-gain,
Sun-day, Mon-day or
al-ways?
If you're sat-is-fied,
I'll be at your side

70

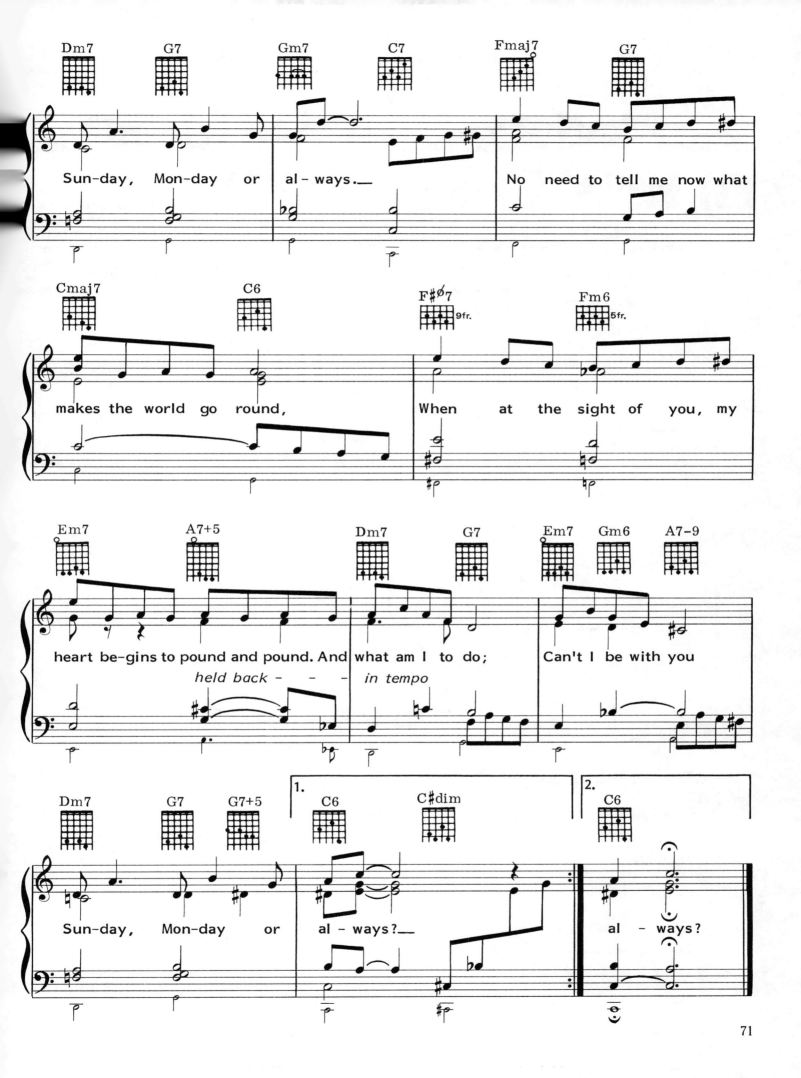

71

I'll Walk Alone

from *Follow the Boys*

Words by Sammy Cahn; Music by Jule Styne

Dinah Shore introduced "I'll Walk Alone" in the 1944 film Follow the Boys. *It is one of the definitive love songs of World War II, expressing the mood of the nation as well as any other tune of*

the era did. Like "Ac-cent-tchu-ate the Positive" (see page 60), it was nominated for an Academy Award for 1944 but lost to "Swinging on a Star." Songwriters Jule Styne and Sammy Cahn had already hit the jackpot two years earlier with one of their first collaborations, "I've Heard That Song Before." The team quickly became associated with Frank Sinatra, for whom they wrote "The Charm of You," "I Fall in Love Too Easily," "Time After Time" and a number of other hits. Interestingly, Styne had written another "walk" song three years earlier with lyricist Frank Loesser — "I Don't Want to Walk Without You."

My Foolish Heart

from *My Foolish Heart*   Words by Ned Washington; Music by Victor Young

"My Foolish Heart" first appeared as the title song of a 1949 tearjerker starring Dana Andrews and Susan Hayward, who was, with the possible exception of Barbara Stanwyck, the greatest film crier of her time. The Victor Young-Ned Washington song was nominated for an Academy Award and made the No. 1 spot on Your Hit Parade *via a recording by Billy Eckstine. Composer Young was a true musical renaissance man. He began his career as a concert violinist and achieved great success as a songwriter and arranger, scoring more than 350 films before his death in 1956. Among his most famous compositions are "Love Letters," "When I Fall in Love," "Golden Earrings," "Around the World" and "Street of Dreams." As if all that weren't enough, Young also served as a musical director at Decca Records, working with such veterans as Peggy Lee and helping develop such young singers as Jeri Southern.*

Billy Eckstine

Slowly and romantically

mp flowing

The

C   Am   Dm7   G9   G7-9

night___ is like a love-ly tune, Be - ware,___ my fool-ish heart! How

sim.

Cmaj7   Am   Dm7   Dm7/G

white___ the ev-er-con-stant moon, Take care,___ my fool-ish heart! There's a

from *Tammy and the Bachelor*

**Words and Music by Jay Livingston
and Ray Evans**

*In late August 1957, "Tammy," from the
film* Tammy and the Bachelor *starring
Debbie Reynolds, became the No. 1 hit
in the country. "Tammy," bless her heart,
stayed on the charts for the next eight
months. In all, over 10 million copies of
the tune were sold by dozens of*

TAMMY

Debbie Reynolds

*different performers, with Debbie's own
recording selling more than a million. It
all started with Debbie ("Tammy")
pursuing bachelor Leslie Nielsen after
nursing him back to health following a
plane crash. In 1961, our girl returned,
with Sandra Dee doing the honors, in*
Tammy Tell Me True. *Miss Dee reprised
the role two years later in* Tammy and the
Doctor. *And finally, in 1967, we even
had a TV pilot called* Tammy and the
Millionaire. *Quite a busy young lady.*

Slow, gentle waltz

from *Sweet Rosie O'Grady*

Words by Mack Gordon
Music by Harry Warren

My Heart Tells Me

Betty Grable

Betty Grable supposedly once said: "I can't sing; I can't dance. I can only do one thing — be a star." She displayed that particular talent clearly when she introduced this tune in 1944 in Sweet Rosie O'Grady, first singing it in a bathtub and then later in a beer hall. The song's composers, Harry Warren and Mack Gordon, began writing together in 1940 after extended partnerships with others: Warren with Al Dubin and Gordon with Harry Revel. Besides "My Heart Tells Me," which was a big hit for Glen Gray and the Casa Loma Orchestra, with a vocal by Eugenie Baird, the Warren-Gordon team produced a string of other successes, including "Down Argentina Way," "Chattanooga Choo Choo," "I Know Now," "At Last," "I Had the Craziest Dream," "You'll Never Know" (an Academy Award winner), "Serenade in Blue" and many others.

Moderate and smooth in 2 (♩=1 beat)

My heart tells me this is just a fling;____ Yet you say our love means ev – 'ry – thing.____ Do you mean what you are say – ing, Or is this a lit-tle game you're play – ing?

Only Forever

from *Rhythm on the River*

Bing Crosby and Mary Martin

Words by Johnny Burke; Music by James V. Monaco

"Only Forever" was introduced in Rhythm on the River, a 1940 Paramount musical starring Bing Crosby, Mary Martin and Basil Rathbone and directed by Victor Schertzinger. In the film, Bing and Mary are ghostwriting songs for Basil, and Mary, inspired by Bing's music, "writes" a lyric that consists of four questions all answered by two words: "Only forever." The movie song was actually composed by Jimmy Monaco, who first started writing

for Bing in 1936. Along with lyricist Johnny Burke, he contributed to the scores for a number of Crosby films, including Dr. Rhythm, Sing You Sinners, The Star Maker, If I Had My Way, Rhythm on the River and Road to Singapore. "Only Forever" earned Monaco his first Academy Award nomination (it lost to "When You Wish Upon a Star" from Walt Disney's Pinocchio) and was on Your Hit Parade for several months.

Section 3 HITS FROM THE '30s THAT BECAME HITS AGAIN

Words by Irving Kahal

I Can Dream, Can't I?

Music by Sammy Fain

"I Can Dream, Can't I?" was introduced in a 1938 musical, Right This Way, *by the singer known only as Tamara. It was a million-selling hit 11 years later for The Andrews Sisters. Composer Sammy Fain is one of the underappreciated — though certainly not unsung — stars of American popular song. With Irving Kahal, with whom he worked from the mid-'20s until Kahal's death in 1942, Fain produced a series*

of standards, including "When I Take My Sugar to Tea," "You Brought a New Kind of Love to Me" and "I'll Be Seeing You," which, like "I'll Walk Alone," was one of the prototypical World War II songs. With other lyricists, Fain's hits include "That Old Feeling," "April Love" and two Academy Award winners, both written with Paul Francis Webster, "Secret Love" (1953) and "Love Is a Many-Splendored Thing" (1955).

The Andrews Sisters

Slowly, with expression

I Can Dream, Can't I?

Walkin' My Baby Back Home

Words and Music by Roy Turk, Fred E. Ahlert and Harry Richman

Fred Ahlert and Roy Turk, who were principally Tin Pan Alley songwriters — as opposed to Broadway or Hollywood — turned out some very handsome tunes together, including "Walkin' My Baby Back Home," "I'll Get By," "Mean to Me," "Where the Blue of the Night (Meets the Gold of the Day)" and a too-often-overlooked lovely called "I'll Follow You." "Walkin' My Baby Back Home" was first popularized by one of the great song-and-dance men of the 1920s and '30s. His name was Harry Richman, and while the theater and movies weren't his metiers, in nightclubs few entertainers could touch him. Nearly a quarter of a century later, the song was made famous again by a young man from Oregon who set the country afire for a couple of years just before the advent of rock 'n' roll. Indeed, Johnnie Ray may have helped to usher rock 'n' roll in. His wild, abandoned — and tearful — caterwauling and arm thrashing earned him the title Prince of Wails. But after several hits, including "Cry" and "The Little White Cloud That Cried" ("Walkin' My Baby Back Home" was his only fairly cheerful success), Ray descended almost as abruptly as he had arrived. The Prince was gone. Elvis was now King.

Lighthearted swing

Gee, it's great, af-ter be-in' out late,— Walk-in' my ba - by back home.
Gee, it's great, af-ter be-in' out late,— Walk-in' my ba - by back home.

Arm in arm, o-ver mead-ow and farm,— Walk-in' my ba - by back home.
Arm in arm, o-ver mead-ow and farm,— Walk-in' my ba - by back home.

Life Is

Words
and Music
by
Lew Brown
and
Ray Henderson

It was Ethel Merman who introduced this song in George White's Scandals of 1931. Miss Merman had made her epic stage debut the prior season in Girl Crazy, in which she held the high C note in "I Got Rhythm" for 16 bars, half a chorus, while the orchestra played the melody. She recorded "Life Is Just a Bowl of Cherries," as did Rudy Vallee, and, in one of the earliest attempts at recording a Broadway score, Bing Crosby and The Boswell Sisters sang it — and other hits from the 1931 Scandals — on both sides of a 12-inch Brunswick record. The song had a resurgence of popularity in the mid-1950s, via a recording by singer Jaye P. Morgan.

Just a Bowl of Cherries

Ethel
Merman

90

HEARTACHES

Words by John Klenner
Music by Al Hoffman

Back in the glorious Big Band Era (roughly 1935 to 1945), a good many of the orchestras were "Chicago bands," working in and out of the Windy City from places like the Aragon and Trianon ballrooms, the Marine Dining Room of the Edgewater Beach Hotel and the Blackhawk Restaurant. One of those bands was led by Ted Weems, whose young vocalists were Perry Como and Marvel (her real name, which Hollywood later changed to Marilyn) Maxwell. The Weems band recorded "Heartaches" in the mid-'30s with a pseudo-Latin beat, but nothing happened. Then, in 1947, a disc jockey found the recording in his station's 78-rpm archives and started playing it. Others picked it up, and the song became a hit. Elmo Tanner did the whistling on the record, and the maracas were played by a singer who was just launching an apparently unending career — Perry Como.

Perry Como

South of the Border
(Down Mexico Way)

Words and Music by Jimmy Kennedy and Michael Carr

"South of the Border," a song about Mexico written by two Englishmen, gave its name to a 1939 movie starring the king of the singing cowboys, Gene Autry, who also recorded it. Today, royalties from that multimillion-seller would seem small potatoes to Autry, whose possessions include the California Angels baseball team and a chain of television and radio stations. In the early 1950s, "South of the Border" was one of Frank Sinatra's first recordings for Capitol after he switched labels from Columbia. That recording was arranged by Nelson Riddle, who went on to provide the fine touch and excellent taste that would be a major factor in much of Sinatra's best work.

* Small notes indicate alternate vocal pitches.

South of the Border (Down Mexico Way)

Until the Real Thing Comes Along

Words and Music by Mann Holiner,
Alberta Nichols, Sammy Cahn,
Saul Chaplin and
L. E. Freeman

Among the several writers of this song, we find a name that has had as much staying power as any in the history of American popular music. That name is Cahn — as in Sammy Cahn. Sammy must have known that he was destined to become a towering figure in his chosen profession. Early on, he changed his name from Kahn to Cahn because he didn't want to be confused with another songwriter, Gus Kahn — just one indication of the disarming chutzpah that has always been part of his charm. Sammy's early successes, before teaming up with Jule Styne and later Jimmy Van Heusen, were written with Saul Chaplin. The two created hits primarily for the big bands — Jimmie Lunceford's, Tommy Dorsey's and, in the case of "Until the Real Thing Comes Along," a Kansas City orchestra, Andy Kirk and His Clouds of Joy, featuring the great Mary Lou Williams on piano.

Slow and pretty

I'd work for you; I'd slave for you; I'd be a beg-gar or a knave for you. If that is-n't love,— It will have to do Un-til the real thing comes a-long. I'd glad-ly move the

Words and Music by Walter Donaldson

This song was first popularized in 1930 by Guy Lombardo and His Royal Canadians, became a hit for Tommy Dorsey and Frank Sinatra in the early '40s, and had its greatest success in 1948 through a million-selling recording by Dick Haymes. Walter Donaldson was a prolific, vastly underrated compos-

Little White Lies

er. During his career (which began before World War I and ended in 1947, when he died at the age of 54), he teamed up with many lyricists — Gus Kahn, Johnny Mercer and Harold Adamson among them. ("Little White Lies" is one of the few songs for which he wrote both the words and the music.) These collaborations resulted in such standards as "My Buddy," "Carolina in the Morning," "Yes Sir, That's My Baby," "My Blue Heaven," "Makin' Whoopee," "Love Me or Leave Me" and "You're Driving Me Crazy!"

Stormy Weather

(Keeps Rainin' All the Time)

Words by Ted Koehler; Music by Harold Arlen

"Stormy Weather" is one of the great American popular songs. Though Harold Arlen and Ted Koehler originally wrote it for Cab Calloway in 1933, it was Ethel Waters who sang it in the Cotton Club Revue *at the famed Harlem nightspot that year. "Stormy Weather" quickly became her song. Singing it, she wrote in her autobiography, proved to be a turning point in her life. Later, it also became strongly associated with Lena Horne, who first recorded it in 1941 and sang two different renditions of it in her one-woman Broadway show in the early 1980s. The song is unique in its construction, with two extra measures added in the second and fourth sections. Arlen commented on the unusual structure: "It fell that way. I didn't count the measures till it was all over. That was all I had to say and the way I had to say it." Today, even after countless performances, "Stormy Weather" remains fresh and still speaks volumes. Mr. Arlen said it just right.*

* played

PRISONER OF LOVE

Words by Leo Robin; Music by Russ Columbo

Crooner Russ Columbo introduced "Prisoner of Love" in 1931, sharing the writing credit with Leo Robin. Another crooner, Perry Como, revived the song 15 years later. In 1942, after six years with Ted Weems' band, Como had returned to his hometown of Canonsburg, Pennsylvania, determined to follow his original profession, barbering. But a year later, an agent lined him up with a deal he couldn't refuse — a CBS radio show and an RCA recording contract. Perry went on to turn out hit after hit, including "Till the End of Time," "Because," "Temptation" and his blockbuster version of "Prisoner of Love."

Words by Carroll Loveday
Music by Helmy Kresa

THAT'S MY DESIRE

A man named Helmy Kresa wrote the melody of "That's My Desire" in 1931. It turned out to be his only hit. But then, Kresa wasn't primarily a songwriter. For many years he was the musical arranger for none other than Irving Berlin (whose genius was coupled with minimal ability on the piano and understanding of chord structure). Later, Kresa also became the professional manager of Berlin's publishing company. "That's My Desire" made

a star of a highly stylized singer from Chicago named Frankie Laine, who pursued fame for a dozen years before he finally caught up with it (or it caught up with him). Frankie found the song while working in a defense plant in Cleveland during World War II. He wandered into a little club one night and heard a lady singing the by-then-forgotten tune in a sultry, bluesy way. He recorded the number in 1947, and the best-selling disc changed his life. Unfortunately, his attempts to find the singer in order to thank her proved fruitless.

Frankie Laine

A Little Bit Independent

Words by Edgar Leslie; Music by Joe Burke

Through the years, there have been many songs written either about New York City or at least mentioning The Big Apple in the lyrics. (There probably would have been a lot more but for the fact that there isn't much — an exception is Mamie O'Rourke — that even comes close to rhyming with "New York.") In "A Little Bit Independent," however, lyricist Edgar Leslie added a touch of a New York accent and came up with "A little bit independent in your walk, / A little bit independent in your talk, / There's nothing like you in Paris or New York." The rhyme works especially well in the big city itself, where the true "New Yalker" doesn't pronounce the letter r in words. The song was introduced by Fats Waller in 1935 and recorded in the late '40s first by Dick Haymes and later by Georgia Gibbs with Bob Crosby's orchestra. It was successfully revived in the early '50s by both Nat King Cole and Eddie Fisher. Besides "A Little Bit Independent," Leslie and Joe Burke got together on such other hits as "Moon Over Miami," "On Treasure Island," "In a Little Gypsy Tearoom" and the World War II song "We Must Be Vigilant."

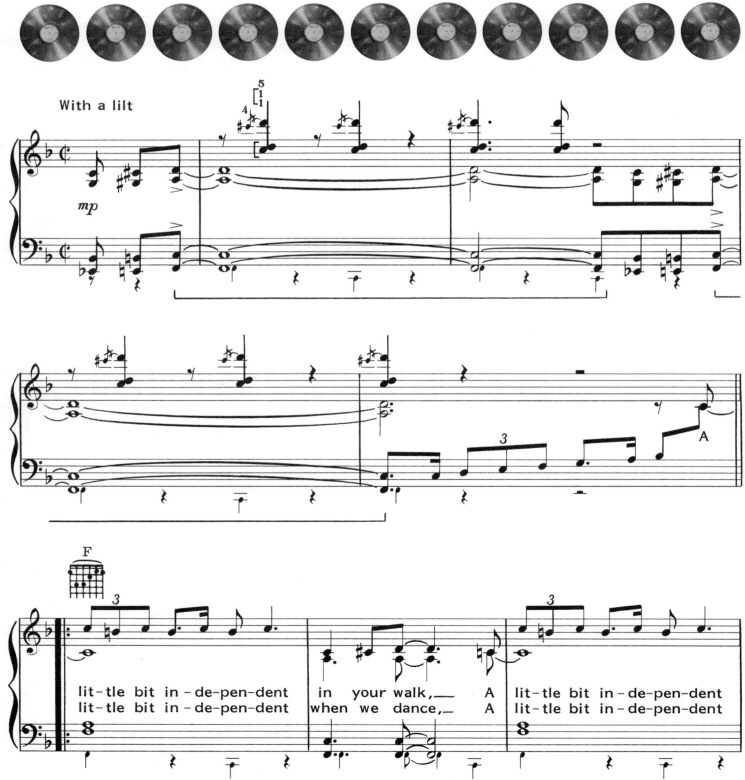

lit-tle bit in-de-pen-dent in your walk,___ A lit-tle bit in-de-pen-dent
lit-tle bit in-de-pen-dent when we dance,___ A lit-tle bit in-de-pen-dent

A Little Bit Independent

Nevertheless

(I'm in Love with You)

Words and Music by
Bert Kalmar and Harry Ruby

One of the great songwriting teams — lyricist Bert Kalmar and composer Harry Ruby — wrote "Nevertheless" in 1931. Their collaboration, begun in 1916, spanned the early days of vaudeville through the Broadway musicals of the 1920s, into the beginnings of the film musical in the '30s and ended only with Kalmar's death in 1947. In 1928, the duo collaborated with The Marx Brothers on the stage version of Animal Crackers and soon found themselves in Hollywood. Two years later, they wrote the first of their many hit film songs, "Three Little Words." Among their best-known songs are "Who's Sorry Now?," "I Wanna Be Loved by You," "A Kiss to Build a Dream On" and "Thinking of You." Fred Astaire and Red Skelton portrayed the pair in the 1950 MGM musical biography Three Little Words. And a year later, Oscar Hammerstein II revised and retitled one of their songs, originally called "Moonlight on the Meadows." As "A Kiss to Build a Dream On," it earned Kalmar and Ruby their final Academy Award nomination.

With an easy swing

May-be I'm right___ and may-be I'm wrong,___ And may-be I'm weak___ and may-be I'm strong,___ But nev-er-the-less___ I'm in love with you.

May-be I'll win___ and

Your Feet's Too Big

Words and Music by Ada Benson and Fred Fisher

"Your Feet's Too Big" was made a hit by one of the great characters of American popular music — Thomas "Fats" Waller. (So closely is the song associated with Fats and his recording of it that Dan Fox based this arrangement on the record.) Born in Harlem in 1904, Waller learned to play the organ at the Abyssinian Baptist Church, where his father preached. At 15, he took first prize in a contest for amateur pianists, and upon graduating from high school he got his first job, as a console player at the Lincoln Theatre on 135th Street. Though Fats was an accomplished pianist, organist and performer, it was as a composer that he made his greatest mark. Among his songs are

"Ain't Misbehavin' " (his biggest hit, which he reportedly wrote in 45 minutes), "Honeysuckle Rose" (he took the lyrics over the phone and came up with the melody within the hour), "The Joint Is Jumpin'," "I've Got a Feelin' I'm Fallin' " and "Keepin' Out of Mischief Now." (But Ada Benson and Fred Fisher supplied him with "Your Feet's Too Big.") Fats had many other talents as well. Louis Armstrong described him as the funniest man he had ever met, and he lived faster and harder than most people. He died in 1943, at the age of 39, but as the saying goes, "There are 39-year-olds and there are 39-year-olds." He and his work were immortalized in the late-1970s hit musical Ain't Misbehavin'.

Fats Waller

Moderate bounce

mf

G7   Dm7   C#dim   G7

Up in Har - lem at a ta - ble for two,___ There were
girl she likes you___ and thinks you are nice.___ You

C   Dm7   C/E   F   C/E   Ebdim

four of us, me, your big feet and you.___ From
got___ what it takes to be in par - a - dise.___ She

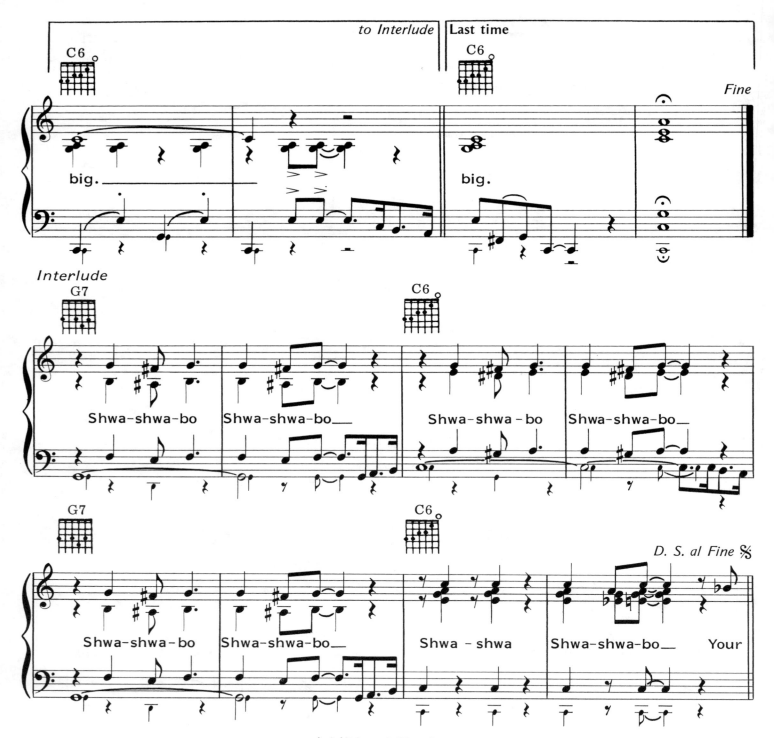

Additional Words

When you go and die, a body will sob;
That old undertaker will have quite a job.
You'll look mighty funny when you lay in that casket,
Your feet stickin' out that basket.
CHORUS and INTERLUDE

Section 4
HITS FROM THE GREAT BAND ERA

Words by
Johnny Burke

IMAGINATION

Music by
Jimmy Van Heusen

"Imagination," a 1940 hit for Glenn Miller and His Orchestra on a Bluebird recording, was one of the earliest collaborations by the songwriting team of Johnny Burke and Jimmy Van Heusen. It was also one of the few times when the songwriters weren't writing for a film or for a stage show but were simply turning out a pop song. In 1941, the two began a 10-year association with Bing Crosby that was quite unlike anything the popular music world had ever seen. They reportedly wrote more than 75 songs for Crosby during that period, songs that

Glenn Miller

virtually defined the singer as we think of him today. The best of these, whether ballads such as "Moonlight Becomes You," "It Could Happen to You" and "But Beautiful," or rhythm numbers such as "Road to Morocco," "Swinging on a Star" and "Aren't You Glad You're You," capture so much of the Crosby character we have come to know — the warmth, the humility, the gentleness, the almost romantic diffidence. That rare understanding and empathy between songwriters and singer is something we'll probably never see the likes of again.

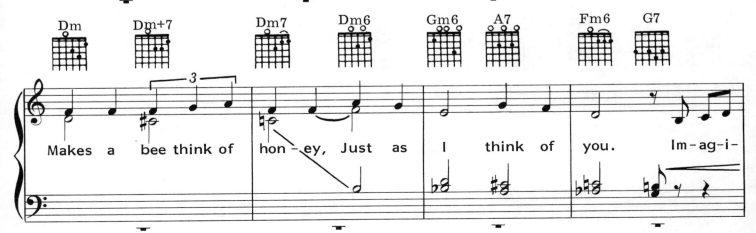

Words by Jack Lawrence; Music by Arthur Altman

Frank Sinatra together with Harry James recorded "All or Nothing at All" in 1940, with only modest success. Then, in the summer of 1943, in the middle of the singer's Paramount days and the ban on recording called by the musicians' union, that same record was revived and sold more than a million copies. Since then, "All or Nothing at All" has remained one of the most popular numbers in Sinatra's repertoire. He recorded it again in 1961 with Don Costa and in 1967 with Nelson Riddle. In 1977, Sinatra even cut a disco version of the song which was intended to be the flip side of his disco "Night and Day" but was never released.

All or Nothing at All

Moderately in 2 (♩ = 1 beat)

All _____ or noth-ing at all!
All _____ or noth-ing at all!

Half a love
If it's love,

_____ nev - er ap - pealed to me. _____
_____ there is no in - be - tween. _____

If your heart _____
Why be - gin, then

_____ nev - er could yield to me, _____
cry for some-thing that might have been. _____

Then I'd rath - er have
No, I'd rath - er have

Music, Maestro, Please!

Words by Herb Magidson; Music by Allie Wrubel

When Tommy and Jimmy Dorsey broke up the Dorsey Brothers Band after their legendary fight on the bandstand at the Glen Island Casino in New Rochelle, New York, in 1935, Tommy took over what had basically been the Joe Haymes orchestra. Haymes was an excellent arranger but never quite made it as a bandleader. Tommy's vocalists in those long-ago pre-Frank Sinatra/Pied Piper days were Edythe Wright and Jack Leonard. Edythe was the singer on "Music, Maestro, Please!," which became a No. 1 hit for the Dorsey organization in the summer of 1938. She left the band the following year, in October, and ultimately was replaced by Connie Haines, along with The Pied Pipers and the great Jo Stafford. Jack Leonard, who at times almost sounded as if he were whispering or cooing — but with intimate and effective results — left that November after a spat with Tommy while the band was performing at the Palmer House in Chicago. He was replaced three months later by Sinatra. Alas, neither Jack nor Edythe ever recaptured their glory days with Dorsey.

waltz. — She danced di- vine- ly, And I loved her so,— But
there I go.— To- night ———— I must- n't think of her,—
No more mem - o - ries. Swing out,———— To- night I
must for - get, Mu- sic, maes- tro, please!

127

I'm Beginning to See the Light

Words and Music by Harry James,
Duke Ellington, Johnny Hodges and Don George

Throughout the Big Band Era, a song written by a member of an orchestra was often credited not only to the composer but to his bandleader and sometimes even to the music publisher as well. A prime example is this 1945 hit, which credits no fewer than four collaborators — Duke Ellington, his star alto saxophonist Johnny Hodges, Don George and Harry James. Each had a hand in the song. Ellington worked on the melody; George wrote the lyrics; and James' orchestra had the big hit with it. But a rule of thumb was that if Hodges got a credit on a tune, you could figure he had pretty substantial input. The joke in the Ellington band was that when Johnny would whip off a gorgeous phrase or chorus while they were playing a blues tune, Duke would write it down, name it and suddenly have himself another song. And "The Rabbit" would sit in the sax section and just glare.

nev-er cared much for moon-lit skies;_ I nev-er wink back at
nev-er went in for af-ter-glow__ Or can-dle-light on the

fire - flies;_ But now that the stars are in your eyes,_ I'm be-
mis-tle-toe,__ But now when you turn the lamp down low,_ I'm be-

gin-ning to see the light. I
gin-ning to see the

light.

129

Memories of You

Words by Andy Razaf
Music by Eubie Blake

Moderately

Ethel Waters introduced "Memories of You," one of the greatest and most enduring American popular songs, in an all-black revue, Blackbirds of 1930. Since then it has been associated with Benny Goodman, Glen Gray and the Casa Loma Orchestra (featuring a spectacular solo by trumpeter Sonny Dunham) and many others. Musicians gravitate to the song because of the beauty, simplicity and logic of Eubie Blake's melody, and Andy Razaf's lovely lyrics almost seem to sing themselves. In a 1983 celebration at Washington, D.C.'s Kennedy Center, honoring Blake's 100th birthday (he died just five days later), singer Joe Williams resurrected another Blake-Razaf evergreen — "I'd Give a Dollar for a Dime." After hearing the song, Eubie reportedly said, "Did I write that? Gee, that's pretty."

Wak-ing skies at sun-rise, Ev-'ry sun-set too, Seems to be bring-ing me Mem-o-ries of you. Here and there, ev-'ry-where, Scenes that we once knew, And they all just re-call

Somebody

In the 1930s and '40s, "Mickey Mouse bands" was a derogatory name for the sugary-sounding members of the Russ Morgan-Sammy Kaye-Kay Kyser-Guy Lombardo-Jan Garber school. A better name might have been Hotel bands, because of their popularity in hotel ballrooms. They played very danceable music and they were entertaining to watch and listen to as well. Russ Morgan, for example, played a trombone so schmaltzily that one could say he had to drain it regularly of chicken fat. His singing was equally caloric. Yet his was a warm, easy-to-listen-to sound. This song, which Russ co-wrote, was his biggest hit.

Else Is Taking My Place

Words and Music by Dick Howard, Bob Ellsworth and Russ Morgan

SLEEPY LAGOON

Words by
Jack Lawrence
Music by Eric Coates

Harry James

"Sleepy Lagoon" has an interesting lineage. English light-classical composer Eric Coates wrote the melody in 1930, and 10 years later, American Jack Lawrence added the lyrics. Tommy Dorsey was the first to popularize the song, via a trombone solo on Red Seal, RCA's classical-music label. In 1942, the song appeared on Your Hit Parade 18 times and became a No. 1 success for Harry James on Columbia. It was one of Harry's first big hits and, along with other performances such as "Ciribiribin," "Two O'Clock Jump" and "The Flight of the Bumble Bee," allowed him to maintain one of the few bands that lasted well past the end of the Big Band Era. Astonishingly, that era, sainted in memory, lasted only 10 years — roughly from 1935 to 1945.

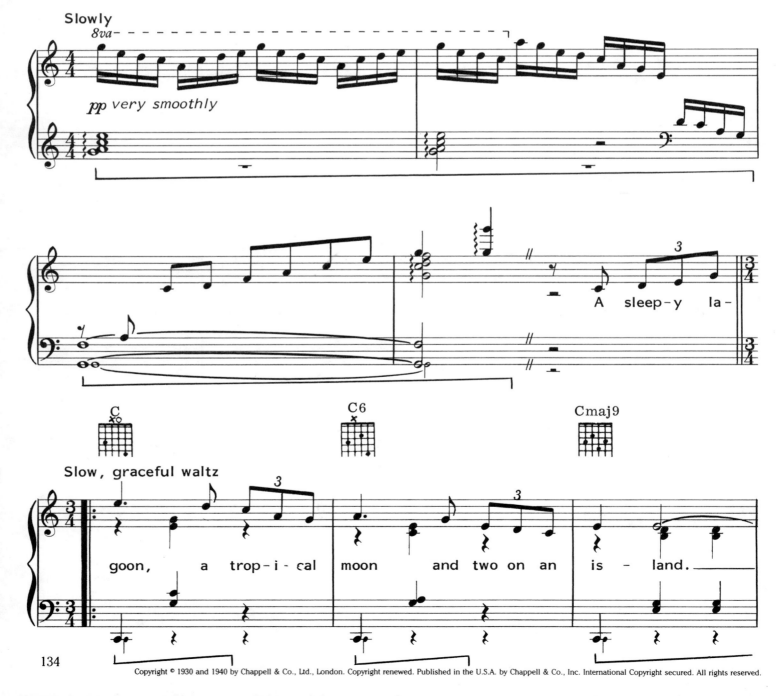

(There Is) No Greater Love

Words by Marty Symes; Music by Isham Jones

"(There Is) No Greater Love" was the last big hit written (in 1936) by another of the under-recognized talents that seem to populate the music field — Isham Jones. As a composer, Jones was responsible for a small but extremely fine list of standards, including "On the Alamo," "Swingin' Down the Lane," "It Had to Be You," "I'll See You in My Dreams" and "The One I Love Belongs to Somebody Else," all featuring lyrics by Gus Kahn. (Marty Symes was his collaborator on "No Greater Love.") As a bandleader, he was the pride of Chicago, working the Green Mill, the Rainbow Gardens and the College Inn. But when the Depression started to empty dance floors, Jones retired to his ranch in California. Some members of his orchestra then formed a cooperative band. At the helm was a young clarinetist who didn't do too badly himself — Woody Herman.

137

UNDECIDED

Words by Sid Robin; Music by Charles Shavers

"Undecided" was introduced in 1939 by Chick Webb and His Orchestra, featuring a vocal by Ella Fitzgerald. It has also been associated with Don Redman and with Benny Goodman, who played it throughout his career, obviously finding its unusual rhythmic feel most interesting. The song, though, had its greatest success in 1951, when The Ames Brothers had a million-selling recording of it. The story behind the title is amusing. Composer Charlie Shavers dropped his tune off with New York music publisher Lou Levy as he was about to go on tour. Levy wired him on the road: "What's the title?" Shavers hadn't thought about one, so wired back: "Undecided." And that's what the name became.

Benny Goodman

First you say you do, And then you don't, And then you say you will, And then you won't. You're un-de-cid-ed now, So

Now you want to play, And then it's no, And when you say you'll stay, That's when you go. You're un-de-cid-ed now, So

EAST OF THE SUN
(and West of the Moon)

In the 1930s, the Ivy League was not only a major force in U.S. college football, but it also occasionally cracked the Top Ten with songs — tunes that were written for the Pennsylvania University Masque and Wig Club and the Princeton Triangle Club shows. (After all, the Ivy League/Tin Pan Alley connection goes back to Cole Porter's writing the "Yale Bulldog Song" in the early part of the century.) The Princeton Triangle show of 1935, Stags at Bay, contained the longest-lasting and loveliest of these collegiate tunes, "East of the Sun (and West of the Moon)," written by a very talented young man named Brooks Bowman. It was a great misfortune of the music world that Bowman was killed in a car crash in 1937 at the age of 24. "East of the Sun" enjoyed its greatest success in 1940, when Tommy Dorsey recorded it with Frank Sinatra, using the band as choir, as he had done so successfully a few years earlier with "Marie" and "Who?"

Words and Music by Brooks Bowman

Moderately, in 2 (♩=1 beat)

East of the sun___ And west of the moon,___

We'll build a dream-house___ of love, dear.

Wishing

Buddy DeSylva did it all — songwriting, producing, heading a major film studio. And sometimes he did more than one thing at a time. A case in point is a 1939 film called Love Affair, which starred Charles Boyer and Irene Dunne and this song, "Wishing." (A 1957 remake was entitled An Affair to Remember.) Leo McCarey, the film's director, needed a wistful ballad to enhance the story. On whom did he call? Buddy DeSylva, of course. De-

Sylva, then producing at Fox, had always been a good lyricist, and, in addition to the other two members of the team of DeSylva, Brown and Henderson, he had worked with George Gershwin, Jerome Kern and Victor Herbert, so obviously he knew his way around a melody. Several bands were successful with this tune, but many people remember Skinnay Ennis singing it on Bob Hope's Pepsodent radio show and putting his stamp on it.

Words and Music by B. G. DeSylva

146

I've Heard That Song Before

Words and Music by Jule Styne and Sammy Cahn

By 1940, Jule Styne had been a vocal arranger and singing coach at 20th Century-Fox for some time. Tiring of his routine and confident that he could write songs with the best of them, he approached Darryl Zanuck, the head of the vast studio. Just at that time, however, Zanuck had announced a halt on musicals. After fulfilling his Fox contract by going on the road as coach and accompanist with actress Constance Bennett, Styne signed on with Republic Studios, known primarily for "oaters" starring Gene Autry, Roy Rogers and other Western heroes. But sometimes the company turned out cheap musicals such as the 1942 film Youth on Parade, which Jule was assigned to write with a man he had never met, a struggling young lyricist named Sammy Cahn. When the two were introduced, Styne was busy plucking out a melody. Years later, Sammy recounted that the first sentence he uttered to the sensitive composer almost ended their association before it began. What he said was, "It seems to me I've heard that song before." Well, the mere suggestion of plagiarism is enough to incite the mildest-mannered songwriter to riot, and Styne exploded. It took Sammy some time to explain that he meant that the last five words of his sentence should be the title of the tune that Jule was working on. It was the beginning of a beautiful — and most profitable — friendship.

149

Amapola

(Pretty Little Poppy)

Words by Albert Gamse
Music by Joseph M. Lacalle

No other band was built around its singers as much as Jimmy Dorsey's. And that was by accident. Furthermore, his singers, Bob Eberly and Helen O'Connell, had been with the band for several years when that accident happened. In 1939, Jimmy took on a radio series for Raleigh cigarettes. (In those days, cigarette companies were big big-band sponsors.) It was only a 15-minute show, and one of Dorsey's arrangers, Tutti Camarata, worked out a plan to feature both singers. He would take a song, slow it down as a ballad for Bob, then speed it up and let Helen swing it. The formula was an immediate success. "Amapola" was their first hit and was followed by many others, including "Green Eyes" and "Brazil." Eberly was perhaps the most popular of all the big-band singers, Frank Sinatra included, with a rich, romantic baritone that won him most of the band-singer polls of 1939-42. It was his misfortune to be drafted into the Armed Forces at the peak of his career, just after filming* The Fleet's In, *in which he scored on "Tangerine" with Helen and on "I Remember You" with Dorothy Lamour. When Bob returned from the war, Sinatra, Dick Haymes and Perry Como had left the bands they sang with and become big singing stars on their own. Eberly found himself largely forgotten.*

Jimmy Dorsey with Bob Eberly and Helen O'Connell

Moderate Latin feel

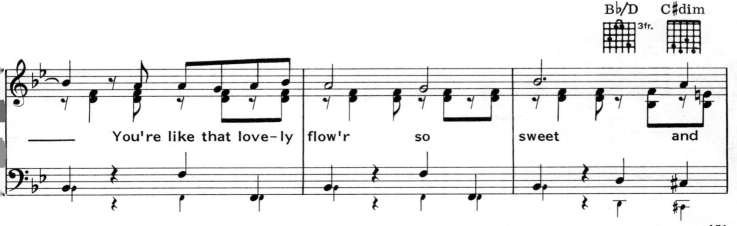

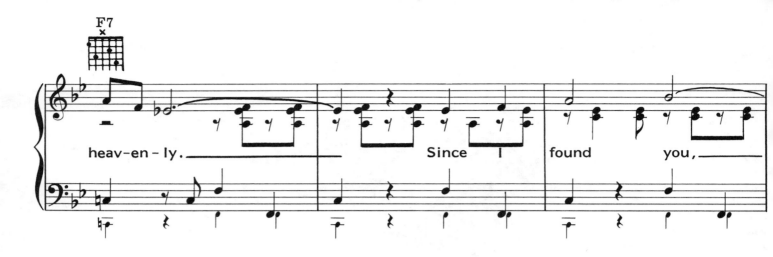

heav-en-ly._____ Since I found you,_____

_____ My heart is wrapped a-round you,_____ And lov-ing you it

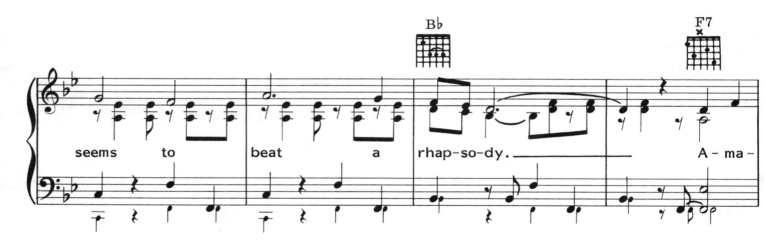

seems to beat a rhap-so-dy._____ A-ma-

po - la,_____ The pret-ty lit-tle pop - py_____

OUR LOVE

Words and Music by Larry Clinton, Buddy Bernier and Bob Emmerich

In 1938, Larry Clinton adapted French composer Claude Debussy's "Reverie" for his band. He called the ballad "My Reverie," and his vocalist, Bea Wain, sang it into the No. 1 spot on Your Hit Parade. *From then on, the classical masters were fair game for Tin Pan Alley. Soon, Maurice Ravel had been tapped for "The Lamp Is Low," Sergei Rachmaninoff for "Full Moon and Empty Arms," Frédéric Chopin for "Till the End of Time" and Peter Ilyich Tchaikovsky for "Moon Love," "Tonight We Love" and others. It was to the Russian master that Clinton turned in 1939 for another No. 1 song. This time, he took his pencil to Tchaikovsky's "Romeo and Juliet* Fantasy Overture." *The result was this lovely song, perhaps the most haunting of all the adaptations.*

Lyrics:

Our love,___ I feel it ev-'ry-where; Through the
Our love___ Is like an eve-ning pray'r; I can

night-time,___ It is the mes-sage of___ the
hear it___ In ev-'ry whis-per of___ the

1. breeze.___

2. trees.

My Devotion

Words and Music by
Roc Hillman and Johnny Napton

Vaughn Monroe

"My Devotion" was a big hit for Vaughn Monroe on Victor Records in 1942. It was the first success for the singer-bandleader, who had been around since the mid-'30s. After a three-year dry spell, he struck gold again in 1945 with "There, I've Said It Again." From then on, it was hit after hit. In the early 1950s, Monroe was so hot that RCA Victor signed him to a long-term contract. But when you're not, you're not. Within a few months of the signing, Vaughn's records abruptly stopped selling. Eventually, the story has it, he worked out his contract by becoming a television pitchman for RCA TV sets. There's no business like show business.

Slowly, with much expression

My de - vo - tion Is end - less and deep as the
My de - vo - tion Is not just a sud - den e -

o - cean And like a star shin - ing from a - far Re -
mo - tion; It will be con - stant - ly burn - ing, And your

157

My Devotion

Words and Music by
Richard Adler and Jerry Ross

In 1950, Mitch Miller went to Columbia Records, and the music business was never quite the same again. The former classical oboist immediately brought his own strong opinions about popular music into play. He believed in "sounds" and songs with simple, to-the-point lyrics. Soon the airwaves were alive with tunes like "Come On-a My House," sung by Rosemary Clooney; "Jezebel," by Frankie Laine; and "Feet Up (Pat Him on the Po-Po)," by Guy Mitchell. This isn't to say that during Miller's long tenure all of Columbia's recordings

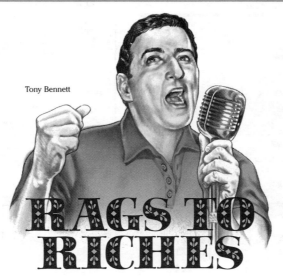

Tony Bennett

RAGS TO RICHES

were novelty tunes. Given the company's connection with the musical theater, Miller recorded many lovely ballads during the 1950s and early '60s. And, to Mitch's credit in many people's eyes, he kept rock 'n' roll from surfacing at Columbia during his reign. One of Miller's protégés was a young Italian-American from New York City who called himself Tony Bennett. The Columbia people — and Tony — were wise in the material they selected for him: "sound" songs to be sure, yet tunes for which he had a special feel, with his rich, romantic baritone. One of these songs was "Rags to Riches," a No. 1 hit for Tony in 1953.

I know I'd go from rags to rich - es
My clothes may still be torn and tat - tered,

If you would on - ly say you care;
But in my heart I'd be a king.

Melody of Love

Words by Tom Glazer; Music by H. Engelmann

"Melody of Love," with lyrics by Tom Glazer, was based on a melody published in 1903 by one H. Engelmann. It became a best-selling instrumental hit in 1955 for Billy Vaughn and His Orchestra on Dot Records and was also a vocal hit for The Four Aces on Decca and for Dinah Shore and Tony Martin on RCA Victor. The song first landed on the charts on January 8, 1955, and a month later hit No. 1, where it remained for six weeks. "Melody of Love," in fact, remained in the Top Ten for nearly six full months. This type of success naturally spawned a series of "cover" records by other artists. One of the most notable of these belonged to Frank Sinatra, who recorded the song with Ray Anthony and His Orchestra while he was with Capitol. It was released as a single (the flip side was "I'm Gonna Live Till I Die") and to this day remains one of the hardest-to-find Sinatra Capitol recordings.

Moderate waltz

CRY

★

Words
and
Music
by
Churchill
Kohlman

Elsewhere in these pages we've talked about that rara avis, the song so big that it provided a hit for more than one artist. But there's an even rarer rara avis in the music business — the single record that provides two hit songs, one on each side of the disc. That happened in 1952 for a young man named Johnnie Ray. "Cry" was on one side of his recording, while one of Johnnie's own tunes, "The Little White Cloud That Cried," was on the other. Furthermore, both songs hit the charts in the same week that January! In less than a month, "Cry" reached No. 1, and its companion soon got as high as No. 4. This was the start of the cliché "He cried all the way to the bank." But as somebody once said, "What's trite is right."

Slowly

If your sweet-heart sends a let-ter of good-bye,_____ It's no se-cret you'll feel bet-ter if you cry._____ When wak-ing from a bad dream, Don't you some-times think it's real? But it's on-ly false e-mo-tions that you feel!_____ If your

Frankie Carle

Pianist Frankie Carle, one of the composers of "Oh! What It Seemed to Be," had one of the best-selling recordings of it, in 1946, with his daughter, Marjorie Hughes, as vocalist. And one of the great show-business stories revolves around George Weiss, who collaborated on the song with Carle and Bennie Benjamin. After the trio had finished the tune, Weiss's publisher managed to arrange an audition with Frank Sinatra. Although George wasn't really a pianist, the publisher told him that even after he played the first chorus he should continue playing in order to hammer the song home. Off they went to Sinatra's office. With Bennie Benjamin harmonizing, George performed one chorus. At that point, Sinatra called Mannie Sachs, an A&R (Artists and Repertoire) man at Columbia Records, to tell him that he had a great new song and that Sachs should arrange a recording session. The conversation then drifted on . . . and on . . . to other matters. Weiss, meanwhile, continued to pound out the melody as instructed. Eventually, after about 20 minutes, his publisher had to go over to the piano, lift George's hands off the keys, pull him up from the piano bench by his armpits, tell him to say good-bye and lead him out of the room. It was worth it, though. Sinatra recorded "Oh! What It Seemed to Be" in late 1945, and, oh, what a smash it was!

Oh! What It Seemed to Be

Words and Music by Bennie Benjamin, George Weiss and Frankie Carle

166

Oh! What It Seemed to Be

TEACH ME TONIGHT

Words by Sammy Cahn
Music by Gene De Paul

This song marks the first collaboration between lyricist Sammy Cahn and composer Gene De Paul. At the time, Cahn was under contract to Warner Brothers in Hollywood, and the studio had the right of first refusal on the tune. After Warners decided to turn it down, the song finally wound up at a company called Hub Music. "Teach Me Tonight" was originally recorded on Decca by a singer named Janet Brace and sold, according to Sammy, exactly three copies — one bought by Miss Brace, one by Gene De Paul and one by Sammy himself. But The DeCastro Sisters' 1954 recording turned the song into a big hit which was on the charts from November 1954 through February 1955. The song subsequently became one of Cahn's most enduring standards. Among the diverse performers who have recorded it over the years are Jo Stafford, Joe Williams, Erroll Garner, Sammy Davis and many others, including rock singer Phoebe Snow in the '70s. In 1983, Frank Sinatra commissioned Sammy to write a new set of lyrics for "Teach Me Tonight" and another Cahn song, "Until the Real Thing Comes Along" (see page 97), and recorded the two tunes with the new verses. As is usually the case, however, great lyrics are better left alone. We've therefore used Sammy's original wordings in this book.

Nice and easy

mp

Did you say I've got a lot to learn?_____ Well don't think I'm try-ing not to learn. Since this is the per-fect spot to learn, Teach me to -

A Dreamer's Holiday

Words by Kim Gannon; Music by Mabel Wayne

Although female songwriters are now commonplace, that hasn't always been so. Until fairly recently, the field was pretty much a male preserve. The distaff exceptions, however, were major ones. Lyricist Dorothy Fields, for example, had hits ranging through four decades and, shortly before her death in 1974, was represented on Broadway with Seesaw, written with Cy Coleman. Some of Dorothy's bellringers were "On the Sunny Side of the Street," "I'm in the Mood for Love" and the Academy Award-winning "The Way You Look Tonight." Ann Ronell gave us one of the great standards of all time in 1932, with "Willow Weep for

Me." Kay Swift had scored earlier with, among others, "Fine and Dandy." And one of the biggest exceptions to the male-preserve rule was a young woman from Brooklyn who was barely out of her teens when she wrote the two biggest Latin-flavored melodies of the late 1920s, "In a Little Spanish Town" and "Ramona." As if these weren't enough, she gave us "It Happened in Monterey" in 1930. Her name was Mabel Wayne. She added the lovely "A Dreamer's Holiday" to her long list in the late 1940s, and it became a hit for a particularly good singer named Buddy Clark, who died from injuries received in a plane crash in 1949.

Climb a-board a but-ter-fly And take off on the breeze.
Ev-'ry day for break-fast, There's a dish of scram-bled stars,

Let your wor-ries flut-ter by And do the things you please
And for lunch-eon, you'll be munch-in' Rain-bow can-dy bars.

(I Love You)
For Sentimental Reasons

"(I Love You) For Sentimental Reasons" was among Nat King Cole's many hits. He recorded it in 1946, before he concentrated on singing and when he was still playing piano with his trio. For years, the word "sentimental" has been a favorite with songwriters: "I'm Getting Sentimental Over You," "In a Sentimental Mood," "Sentimental Me" and "Sentimental Journey" immedi-

ately come to mind. (Aside from its sentimental value, the word has four syllables and scans well.) "For Sentimental Reasons," with lyrics by Deek Watson of The Ink Spots, made the No. 1 spot on the charts in January 1947 and held that enviable position for more than a month. The song was such a hit that Jo Stafford (as Cinderella Q. Stump) and Red Ingle did a send-up of it called "For Seventy Mental Reasons."

Nat King Cole

Words by Deek Watson; Music by William Best

(I Love You) For Sentimental Reasons

Music by F. D. Marchetti

FASCINATION

F. D. Marchetti wrote this valse tzigane (gypsy waltz) in 1904 as a piano piece, as we've used it here. For years, it was one of the staples of the light-classical repertory, but by the 1950s it was heard less and less often, as the kinds of groups that might play it — string ensembles in restaurants, for example — disappeared. The melody returned to prominence in 1957 when, played by a troupe of violinists, it was the recurring theme in the film Love in the Afternoon. "Fascination" might have faded into oblivion again if New England-born Jane Morgan, who had spent so many years singing in Paris that she was considered a "Continental chanteuse," hadn't had a tremendous hit with it the same year. A nice coincidence for this songbook: Our annotator, Jim Lowe, recorded his one big hit, "Green Door," in the same studio in which Miss Morgan recorded "Fascination." His recording session followed hers by just a few hours. Jim says that he'd be most happy to follow Jane into a studio again, anytime.

Slow, graceful waltz

On a Slow Boat to China

Words and Music by Frank Loesser

Kay
Kyser

"On a Slow Boat to China," written by Frank Loesser, was a hit for Kay Kyser and appeared on the charts for 15 weeks in late 1948 and early 1949. In fact, at one point, Loesser had songs at No. 1 and No. 2 on the charts — this one and "My Darling, My Darling." "On a Slow Boat to China" was later interpolated into the MGM musical Neptune's Daughter (1949) as background music for a bathing-suit fashion-show sequence. The film also featured another Loesser standard, the Academy Award-winning "Baby, It's Cold Outside." Earlier in his career, Loesser had worked in Hollywood as lyricist for many composers, including Hoagy Carmichael, Arthur Schwartz and Jimmy McHugh. How-

ever, during World War II, he began writing music as well as lyrics and in 1948 scored a great success on Broadway with the show Where's Charley? From then on, he devoted himself almost exclusively to the Broadway stage. In 1950, he produced Guys and Dolls, followed by The Most Happy Fella (1956), Greenwillow (1960) and How to Succeed in Business Without Really Trying (1961), for which he received a Pulitzer Prize. Loesser was a true heir to the mantle of Irving Berlin and Cole Porter — the complete songwriter. His death in 1969 at the age of 59 was a tremendous blow to the American musical stage.

On a Slow Boat to China

182

We Three
(My Echo, My Shadow and Me)

Words and Music by Dick Robertson, Nelson Cogane and Sammy Mysels

Unfortunately, "We Three" came out in late 1940, just before ASCAP banned its tunes from being played on the radio. The ban deprived people of their favorite songs for nearly a year and killed off or compromised the popularity of several new ones, including "We Three." But the song, thanks to The Ink Spots' recording, had already received enough air play to reach No. 1 on the eve of the ban and to be played on the nation's tens of thousands of juke-

boxes. The Ink Spots' 1939 recording of "If I Didn't Care" launched them on their tremendous career. Indeed, there are at least two singing groups around who still call themselves by that name — even though the last surviving member of the original foursome, Bill Kenny, died in 1978. Kenny, with his fantastic falsetto tenor, was the star attraction. His high, romantic singing was balanced by a heartfelt spoken interlude, delivered (originally by "Hoppy" Jones and, later, by Bill Kenny's brother Herb) in a bass voice full of despair.

The Ink Spots

Easy swing

We three,___ we're all a- lone, Liv-ing in a mem - o -
ry, My ech-o,___ my shad-ow___ and me.
We three,___ we're not a crowd;

We Three (My Echo, My Shadow and Me)

CANADIAN SUNSET

Words and Music by Eddie Heywood and Norman Gimbel

"Canadian Sunset" is among that rare breed of song — one that sells more than a million copies for two different artists. The year was 1956. The artists were Hugo Winterhalter, who recorded his instrumental on RCA Victor, and Andy Williams, whose vocal version on Cadence was his first big hit. The song was composed by the great jazz pianist Eddie Heywood, who played the piano part on Winterhalter's recording. Eddie has a bad stutter, and, as with Ray Charles, that stutter or stammer some-

times comes out and even permeates his playing. And to great advantage. Eddie had a long association with Billie Holiday. They first recorded together in the late 1930s, and by the early '40s, Eddie had pretty much replaced Teddy Wilson as Lady Day's primary accompanist on records. You can hear them together on countless Columbia and Commodore small-group recordings. Their association ended, on discs at least, when the recording ban by the musicians' union hit in 1942.

The Gypsy

Words and Music by Billy Reid

"The Gypsy" was first popularized by that great WSM and WNEW alumna Fanny Rose Shore — better known as Dinah Shore. It was also a big hit for The Ink Spots on Decca Records. There was one other famous — or, if you prefer, infamous — recording made of the song in 1946. The great bebop alto saxophonist Charlie "Bird" Parker was then working at Billy Berg's Jazz Club in Los Angeles and recorded the tune for Dial Records. At that time, Bird's drug habits were getting the better of him, and in the studio that day he had what amounted to a breakdown. He managed to record two ballads — "The Gypsy" and "Lover Man." Both recordings are available today and are beautiful, frightening and excruciating at the same time. You can almost see the man falling to pieces in front of you. Shortly thereafter, Parker was put into a mental institution. Six months later he emerged a changed man (although his years of addiction eventually caused his death in 1955, at the age of 34), but his rendition of "The Gypsy" remains as a terrifying record of one man's descent into a hell on earth.

Moderately slow

In a quaint car-a-van,— There's a la-dy they call The Gyp-sy.

She can look in the fu-ture And drive a-way all your

Blue Velvet

**Words and Music by
Bernie Wayne and Lee Morris**

"Blue Velvet" was first popularized in 1951 by Tony Bennett. For years, comedians have had a field day with this tune, mimicking Tony's New York accent and ever-so-slight and entirely endearing speech impediment. They somehow manage to turn "She wore blue velvet" into "See woah bwew velvut." Now, decades later, with his singing career going stronger than ever and his paintings (done under his real name, Anthony Benedetto) yielding large amounts of acclaim and income, Tony probably doesn't spend much time brooding about his mimics. "Blue Velvet"

Bobby Vinton

was revived in 1963 with tremendous success on Epic Records, this time by that Polish Prince Bobby Vinton. It proved to be an even greater hit than Tony's version and to this day remains one of the singer's most requested songs. Vinton, at the time, was going against the rock 'n' roll of the era, recording such other smooth ballads as the 1940s' "There, I've Said It Again" and another "blue" song, Burt Bacharach and Hal David's "Blue on Blue." Bobby, by the way, is a product of Canonsburg, Pennsylvania, hometown of another singer of no small repute — Perry Como.

Slowly, with expression

She wore blue vel – vet, Blu – er than vel–vet was the night, Soft – er than sat – in was the light From the stars. She wore blue vel – vet,

My Sugar Is So Refined

Johnny Mercer

"My Sugar Is So Refined," written by the team of Sylvia Dee and Sidney Lippman, was one of those songs that arrive, make a small ripple and then pretty much disappear. The tune had its greatest success in 1946 in the hands of Johnny Mercer, marking one of the few occasions when the lyricist had a hit (though a modest one) with someone else's material. Of course, Mercer's biggest hit with a song that wasn't his own was with "Personality," by Johnny Burke and Jim-

Words by
Sylvia Dee;
Music by
Sidney Lippman

my Van Heusen. "My Sugar Is So Refined" was also recorded by Nat Cole and by The Hi-Lo's. This modest little number can't help but bring to mind other "sugar" songs — "When I Take My Sugar to Tea," "Sugar Blues," "Sugar" and the like. Not the greatest song ever written, far from the worst, it is simply, in its melodic freshness and lyric inventiveness, an example of the good, solid American songwriting craftsmanship of its era. An era that now, sadly, appears to have passed.

Easy swing

My sug-ar is so re-fined;_ She's one o' them
My sug-ar is so re-fined;_ She's one o' them

high-class kind._ She does-n't wear a hat; She wears a cha-peau._ She
high-class kind._ She nev-er says "good-bye"; It's al-ways "fare-well." She

She says "to - mah - to" in- stead of "to - ma - to";___
She says "ba - nah - na" in- stead of "ba - na - na";___

She says "po - tah - to" in- stead of "po - ta - to."___ And you should see___ how she
She says "pi - ah - no" in- stead of "pi - a - no."___ And you should see___ how she

holds a cup of tea, With just two fin - gers while she sticks out three.___
sits on her set - tee With cake and cof - fee bal - anced on one knee.___

My sug - ar is so re - fined;___ She's one o' them
My sug - ar is so re - fined;___ She's one o' them

high-class kind.__ She nev-er shares a kiss; She lets our lips u-nite, But,
high-class kind.__ She acts just like her name Is Mis-sus Van Der Loon, And

oh, it feels like kiss-in', and each kiss is dy-na-mite.
though I love my sug-ar and though we'll be mar-ried soon,

won-der what she thinks of each time I hold her tight?
bet that she'll read Shake-speare the whole darn hon-ey-moon.

Oh, she's so re-fined!

CARELESS

Words and Music by Lew Quadling, Eddy Howard and Dick Jurgens

Eddy Howard

Dick Jurgens

"Careless" came out of Chicago. Although never really a rival of New York with its Tin Pan Alley, the Windy City was in direct competition with Gotham when it came to bands. A number of songs originated with or were written for Chicago-based crews, particularly by Isham Jones for his orchestra in the early 1920s and later by Ted Fiorito, Art Kassel and Dick Jurgens. Jurgens' own band was particularly productive in generating hits, turning out "My Last Goodbye," "Cecilia," "A Million Dreams Ago," "Elmer's Tune" and this song, among others. "Careless" was written by Jurgens, his vocalist, Eddy Howard, and his pianist, Lew Quadling, and became No. 1 in February 1940. Notice the clever word usage at the end of the tune: "Are you just careless as you seem to be, or do you just care less for me?" The song's publisher — none other than Irving Berlin — suggested this twist, which was responsible for making "Careless" a big hit.

In a lazy 4 (but not too slow)

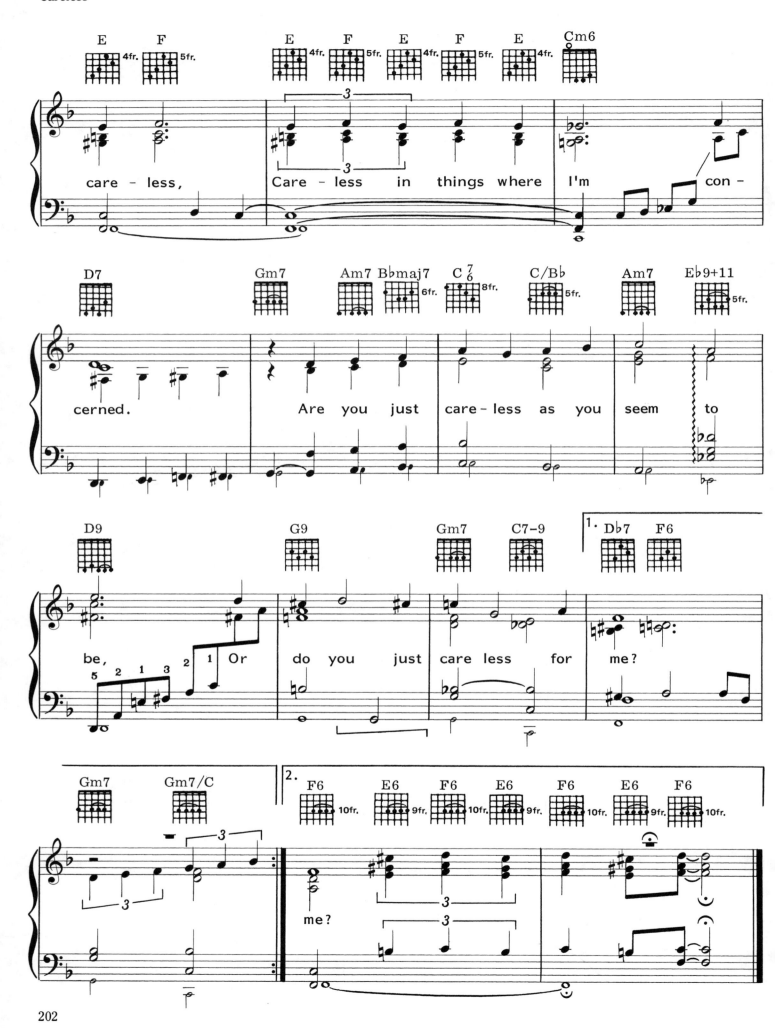

We'll Meet Again

Words and Music by
Ross Parker
and Hughie Charles

"We'll Meet Again," by the English songwriting team of Ross Parker and Hughie Charles, was introduced in 1939 by the British Kate Smith — Vera Lynn. One might go so far as to say of Miss Lynn that, although she didn't win World War II singlehandedly, she certainly made a significant contribution to the effort. The song itself is another of the great ballads of the war years. It could be called a British cousin to such American wartime ballads as "I'll Be Seeing You," "I'll Walk Alone" and the like. Years later, in 1964, the song was to reappear with blistering effectiveness at the end of Stanley Kubrick's black comedy Dr. Strangelove, or How I Learned to Stop Worrying and Love the Bomb. At the end of that film, when the dreaded Doomsday Machine has been activated, triggering a slow-motion, almost balletic, series of nuclear explosions and mushroom clouds, we hear a chorus singing "We'll Meet Again." The effect of the words on the listener is simply overwhelming: "So will you please say hello to the folks that I know, / Tell them I won't be long. / They'll be happy to know that as you saw me go, / I was singing this song."

Moderately, with a strong pulse

We'll meet a - gain, Don't know where, don't know when, But I

know we'll meet a - gain some sun - ny day.

The Glow-Worm

Original words by Lilla Cayley Robinson; Modern words by Johnny Mercer; Music by Paul Lincke

The Mills Brothers

T h i s musical salute to the lightning bug is really two different songs. The original, written in Germany in 1902, was a sprightly little dance tune. Enter, in 1952, The Mills Brothers and Johnny Mercer. "The Glow-Worm," a song based upon the old tune with lyrics by Lilla Cayley Robinson, had long been a favorite of beginning pianists, and that's how the quartet first heard it, played by a little girl at a piano recital. Intrigued with the melody, they asked Mercer, the sentimental gentleman from Georgia and commercial gentleman from Tin Pan Alley, to write new lyrics for it. On the best-selling recording that resulted, The Mills Brothers used both Johnny's breezy modern verses and Miss Robinson's charming though archaic original ones — as we have done here.

Medium jump

1. Glow lit-tle glow-worm, fly of fire;___ Glow like an in-can-
2. Glow lit-tle glow-worm, glow and glim-mer; Swim through the sea of
3. Glow lit-tle glow-worm, turn the key on; You are e-quipped with

(1) des-cent wire;___ Glow for the fe-male of the spe-cie;
(2) night, lit-tle swim-mer; Thou aer-o-nau-ti-cal boll___ wee-vil,
(3) tail-light ne-on. You got a cute vest-pock-et Maz-da,

206

Original Words

Shine little glow-worm, glimmer, (glimmer);   Shine little glow-worm, glimmer, (glimmer);
Shine little glow-worm, glimmer! (glimmer!)   Shine little glow-worm, glimmer! (glimmer!)
Lead us lest too far we wander,   Light the path below, above,
Love's sweet voice is calling yonder!   And lead us on to love!

HONEYSUCKLE ROSE

Words by Andy Razaf; Music by Thomas "Fats" Waller

Fats Waller

Much has been written about Fats Waller, but let's take a moment to talk about his longtime lyricist, Andy Razaf. Andy was born in Washington, D.C., the son of a Malagasy nobleman. In fact, his real name was the exotic Andrea Paul Razafkeriefo. After joining ASCAP as early as 1929, he started working with Waller. The tunes they turned out were just glorious. Some of them, in addition to the one you're looking at, were: "Ain't Misbehavin'," "Keepin' Out of Mischief Now," "Blue Turning Gray Over You" and that early protest song "What Did I Do to Be So Black and Blue." In addition, he wrote the words to "In the Mood" after it became an instrumental hit for Glenn Miller. That was Andy Razaf, another of the many songwriters whose tunes we know but whose name we don't. Alas.

Andy Razaf

Lightly swinging

Ev - 'ry hon - ey - bee / When you're pass - in' by,

Fills with jeal - ous - y / Flow - ers droop and sigh,

When they see you out with me. / And I know the rea - son why;

I don't blame them, / You're much sweet - er,

*8va lower
(piano only)*

BASIN STREET BLUES

Words and Music by Spencer Williams

Give Nobody None of This Jelly Roll." "Basin Street Blues" became famous via a 1931 recording that featured a vocal by the great jazz trombonist Jack Teagarden. The band was The Charleston Chasers, organized for the date by Benny Goodman, with Teagarden and Glenn Miller on trombones. Miller's biographer George T. Simon maintains that Glenn arranged the song and also wrote words and music for what subsequently became the published verse — the part that begins "Won't-cha come along with me" — though he never claimed credit or royalties.

"Basin Street Blues" was written by one of the best and most overlooked early jazz composers — Spencer Williams. Williams, a Louisianan, was a rarity for his time: a black man with a college education. Among his other hits are "Everybody Loves My Baby," "I've Found a New Baby," "I Ain't Got Nobody" and two songs made famous by Louis Armstrong and Bessie Smith — "Mahogany Hall Stomp" and "I Ain't Gonna

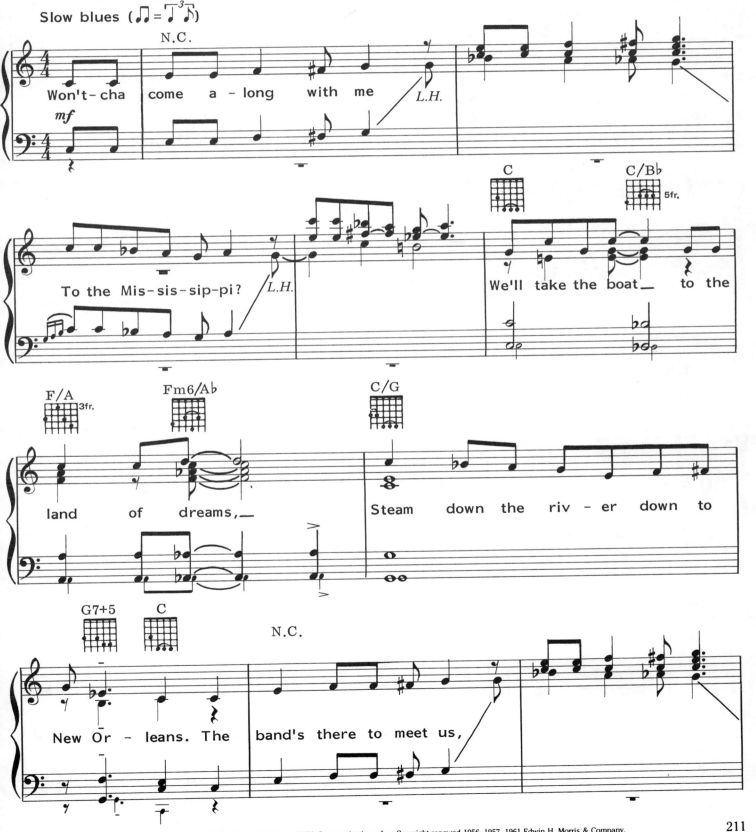

Won't-cha come a-long with me
To the Mis-sis-sip-pi?
We'll take the boat to the
land of dreams,—
Steam down the riv-er down to
New Or-leans. The band's there to meet us,

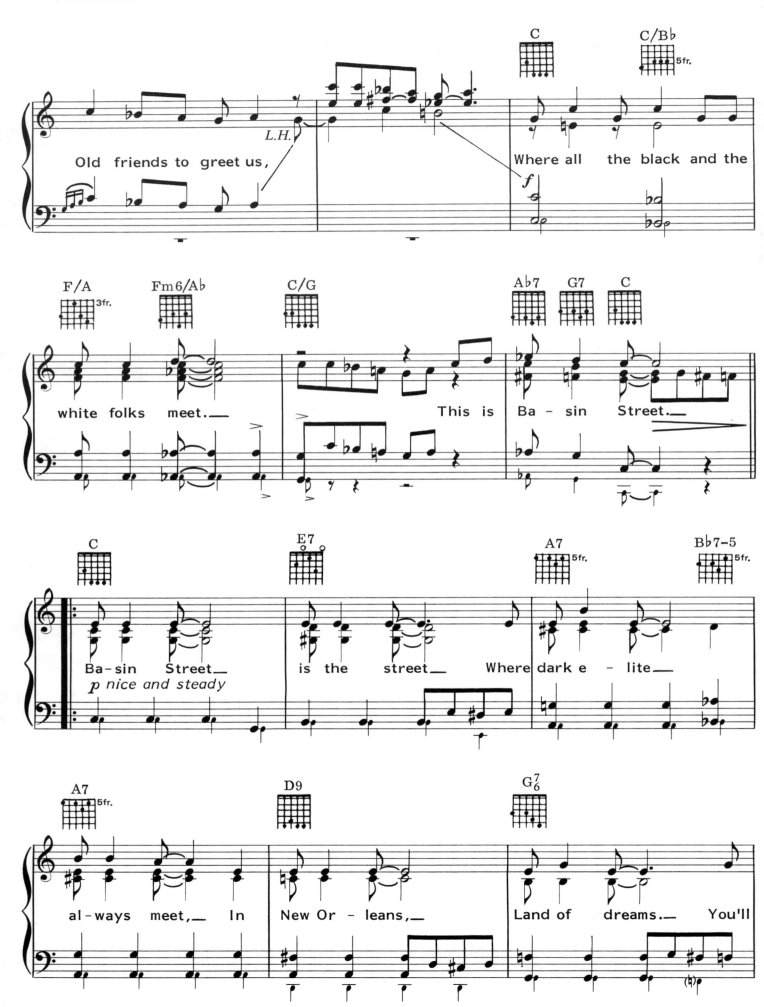

BACK IN YOUR OWN BACK YARD

This song, though with different lyrics and a different title ("It's Nobody's Fault But Mine"), was one of the many introduced by the man who has been called the greatest entertainer of them all — Al Jolson. As "Back in Your Own Back Yard," the revised version was first performed by Paul Ash and His Orchestra at the

Words and Music by
Al Jolson, Billy Rose and Dave Dreyer

New York Paramount. *It is one of the ironies of show business that Jolson, the first person to sing a song in talking pictures and therefore a seminal figure in Hollywood's history, was declared box-office poison by film distributors a few years later and appeared but sparingly in movies afterward. It is a testimonial to his stamina and self-confidence that when they filmed* The Jolson Story *he wanted to play himself, despite the fact that he was getting on in years. However, the role went to Larry Parks, for whom Jolson dubbed on the sound track. But the stage was Jolson's métier, and that's where he sang this song.*

IS IT TRUE WHAT THEY SAY ABOUT DIXIE?

Words and
Music by Irving Caesar,
Sammy Lerner and Gerald Marks

Al Jolson

Like "Back in Your Own Back Yard," "Is It True What They Say About Dixie?" was made popular by Al Jolson, who often sang in black face. Stephen Foster, who wrote so many lovely tunes linked to the South, sojourned there only briefly. On this song, three New York tunesmiths, who perhaps had never ventured south of New Jersey, got themselves off the geographic hook by posing a question about the Southland. One of the writers, Irving Caesar, had peaked in the '20s, contributing the lyrics for such songs as "Swanee" and the score for No, No, Nanette. Caesar was still going strong in 1984. That year, at a big night for songwriters at the Palace Theatre in New York, with such greats as Burton Lane, Johnny Green, Cy Coleman and Jerry Herman in attendance, Caesar, then nearing 90 and with failing vision, stole the show with a spirited performance of his own songs.

Exuberant cakewalk tempo

The Music Goes 'Round and Around

Words by "Red" Hodgson; Music by Edward Farley and Michael Riley

Without any doubt, this was the *nonsense* song of 1935. Introduced and first popularized in a New York nightclub by its composers, Edward Farley and Michael Riley, it is one of those novelty tunes that, even to this day, seem intermittently to come from way out in left field and command attention by their very absurdity. And this one for a while threatened to become a national craze, if not, some thought, a national menace. You might describe "The Music Goes 'Round and Around" as a deliberately silly primer on how the French horn is played. Riley and Farley recorded it for the then newly organized recording company Decca, and the tune was the label's first release to show a profit. It was revived by Danny Kaye in the 1959 film *The Five Pennies*, the story of cornet player Red Nichols. It has also been recorded by many different vocalists, including Ella Fitzgerald and Mel Tormé. Which all just goes to show that sometimes you can't keep a bad song down.

* *Melody note for singers only.*

219

"That Old Gang of Mine" was written in 1923 by the odd triumvirate of Billy Rose, Mort Dixon and Ray Henderson. At the time, Rose was working as a court stenographer for New York City. He collaborated with Dixon on the lyrics (which were inspired by Charles Lamb's famous poem "Old Familiar Faces"), and Henderson later wrote a melody for them. The result was used in The Ziegfeld Follies of 1923, where it proved to be a great hit for the team of Van and Schenck. For several months, sheet-music sales topped 30,000 copies a week. The tune was one of Henderson's first hits and the third hit for Rose. His first came with "You Tell Her, I S-t-u-t-t-e-r," in 1922. The song had a stuttering lyric, and Rose tried a similar device the following year with "Barney Google." "That Old Gang of Mine," a song without gimmicks, gave Rose legitimacy as a lyric writer.

THAT OLD GANG OF MINE

Words and Music by Billy Rose, Mort Dixon and Ray Henderson

222

YOU'RE DRIVING ME CRAZY!

(What Did I Do?)

Words and Music by Walter Donaldson

"You're Driving Me Crazy! (What Did I Do?)" was written by one of the most prolific and successful composers in popular-music history — Walter Donaldson. Today, Donaldson is shockingly little known, but his contribution is enormous. Early in his career, he collaborated extensively with lyricist Gus Kahn, but by the late 1920s he had begun on occasion to write both words and music, as he did here. He originally named the song "What Did You Do to Me?" and turned it over to Guy Lombardo. However, just before Lombardo and His Royal Canadians introduced it, Donaldson revised the title to "You're Driving Me Crazy!" Lombardo played the tune nightly on his radio program, and in no time at all it took off. Today, "You're Driving Me Crazy!" stands as one of Donaldson's most enduring standards and, along with "My Blue Heaven," "At Sundown," "Makin' Whoopee" and "Love Me or Leave Me," ranks among his finest works as a composer and lyricist.

Walter Donaldson

Nagasaki

Words by Mort Dixon
Music by Harry Warren

Bright and spirited

This song contains one of the most memorable of all lines in the long history of American popular music, one so outrageously abrasive and gloriously insane that one wonders what went through the mind of that excellent lyricist Mort Dixon when he wrote "Back in Nagasaki where the fellers chew tobaccy and the women wicky-wacky-woo." The melody was written by Harry Warren. Both Warren and Dixon ended up at Warner Brothers, where the former was paired with the mercurial Al Dubin. In those salad days at the big Burbank studios, theirs was one of the most successful of the Hollywood teams. Although Dixon's career wasn't to be as heady, he did hit pay dirt on several occasions, with scores for such movies as the 1934 Flirtation Walk, *which starred Dick Powell and Ruby Keeler.*

Fel-lows, if you're on, I will spin a yarn That was told to me by a - ble sea - man Jones.
When the day is warm, You can keep in form With a bowl of rice be - neath a par - a - sol.

Once he had the blues, So he took a cruise, Far a-
Ev - 'ry gen-tle- man Has to use a fan, And they

Nagasaki

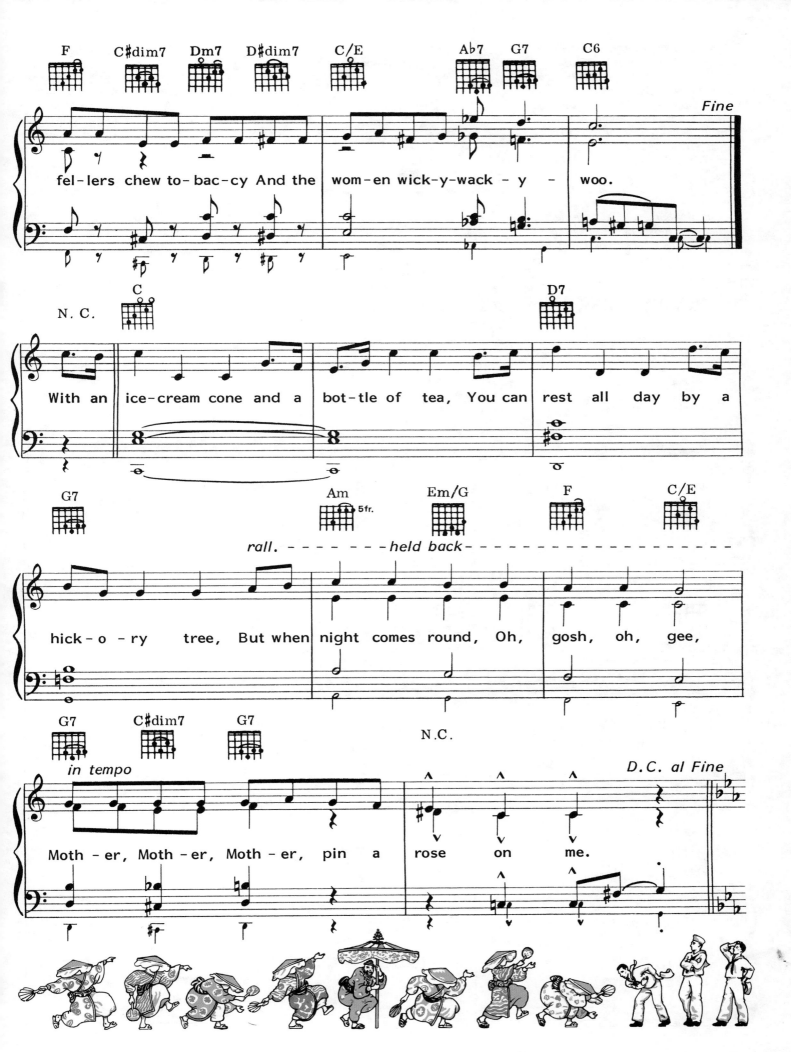

"Baby Won't You Please Come Home" was written by Charles Warfield and Clarence Williams in 1919. It was recorded and made a jazz classic by Jimmie Lunceford, who led what today is perhaps the most unjustly neglected of the great swing bands. It was a band that, alongside Duke Ellington's and Count Basie's groups, ranks as one of the greatest black bands of the Big Band Era. Lunceford, born in Fulton, Missouri, in 1902, earned a bachelor of music degree from Fisk University. In 1926, he became a

music teacher at Manassa High School in Memphis, where he formed his first band, which gained fame on local radio. After the group moved to New York in 1933, an engagement at the Cotton Club drew widespread attention. For years afterward, Lunceford's was the most popular band in Harlem and toured extensively as well. Sy Oliver, Willie Smith, Trummy Young and Paul Webster were among the greats who played with him. He died suddenly in 1947, while touring the Pacific Northwest.

Jimmie Lunceford

Baby Won't You Please Come Home

Words and Music by Charles Warfield and Clarence Williams

A Day in the Life of a Fool

(Manhã de Carnaval)   Words by Carl Sigman; Music by Luiz Bonfa

As "Manhã de Carnaval" (Morning of the Carnival), "A Day in the Life of a Fool" first appeared in the stunning 1959 Academy Award-winning film Black Orpheus. The Brazilian movie is a contemporary retelling of the tragic Greek myth of Orpheus and Eurydice, set against Carnival time in Rio de Janeiro. The film's score was a sneak preview of the bossa nova craze that swept north from Brazil just a few years later. Luiz Bonfa, the composer of this theme and an accomplished guitarist and vocalist, went to New York in 1958 and performed and recorded with the brilliant saxophonist Stan Getz. His mood-filled song, for which Carl Sigman supplied English lyrics, has been recorded often, most notably by Frank Sinatra and Jack Jones.

234

A Day in the Life of a Fool (Manhã de Carnaval)

S·Y·M·P·H·O·N·Y

Original French words by André Tabet and Roger Bernstein;
English words by Jack Lawrence; Music by Alstone

*Johnny Desmond, who had sung with the Glenn Miller Air Force Band, brought
"Symphony" to America from France after World War II. In addition to Johnny's
recording (using Jack Lawrence's English lyrics), the song was waxed by Freddy
Martin and His Orchestra and by a lady who, through the years, has been many
people's favorite singer. Certainly no vocalist ever had better intonation than Jo
Stafford, and, equally certainly, no pop singer had a wider range. Jo first came to the
public's attention as a member of Tommy Dorsey's vocal group The Pied Pipers.
Tommy didn't let her solo very often, but when he did she soared. (Anyone who's heard
her recording of "For You" will know just how high.) Johnny Mercer was one of those listening,
and, after she left Dorsey in 1942, he signed her for Capitol. Jo rewarded his confidence by becoming
one of America's biggest-selling recording artists during the next 10 years. Her 1945 version of
"Symphony" sounds just as good today as it did more than 40 years ago, if not better.*

Jo Stafford

If You Love Me, Really Love Me
(Hymne à l'Amour)
English words by Geoffrey Parsons; French words by Edith Piaf; Music by Marguerite Monnot

Edith Piaf

The French chanteuse Edith Piaf, "The Little Sparrow," introduced "Hymne à l'Amour" (Hymn to Love) to the world in 1949. She had written it with Marguerite Monnot, who also composed "The Poor People of Paris" (see page 243). Piaf's mother, who abandoned her, was an Italian café singer; her father, a circus acrobat. With her frail presence and melancholy songs, including "La Vie en Rose," she became a living metaphor for the disillusionment so rife in France, particularly Paris, in the aftermath of two World Wars. With English lyrics (we've included both the English and French here), her "Hymne" became "If You Love Me, Really Love Me," a hit for Kay Starr in 1954.

If the sun should tum-ble from the sky, If the sea should sud-den-ly run
Le ciel bleu sur nous peut s'é-crou-ler, Et la ter - re peut bien s'ef-fon-

dry, If you love me, real-ly love me, Let it hap-pen, I won't
drer Peu m'im-por-te si tu m'ai-mes, Je me moque du monde en-

care.

If it seems that ev-'ry-thing is lost, I will

tier. *Tant qu'l'a- mour i - non-dra mes ma- tins,* *Que mon*

smile and nev-er count the cost, If you love me, real - ly love me, Let it

corps fré-mi-ra sous tes mains, *Peu m'im-porte les grands pro- blè-mes, Mon a-*

hap-pen, dar-ling, I won't care. Shall I catch a shoot-ing star? Shall I

mour puis-que tu m'ai - mes. *J'- vais jus-qu'au bout du monde, Je me*

bring it where you are? If you want me to, I will. You can

fe - rais tein - dre blonde, Si tu me le de-man-dais. *On peut*

set me an-y task; I'll do an-y-thing you ask, If you'll on-ly love me
bien ri-re de moi, Je fe-rais n'im-por-te quoi, Si tu me le de-man-

still. When at last our life on earth is through, I will
dais. Nous aur-ons pour nous l'é-ter-ni- té, Dans le

share e-ter-ni-ty with you. If you love me, real-ly love me, Then what-
bleu de toute l'im-men-si- té. Dans le ciel plus de pro- blè-mes, Dieu ré-

ev-er hap-pens, I won't care.___ If the care.___
u-nit ceux qui s'ai - ment.___ Le ciel ment.___

Words by Jack Lawrence
Music by Marguerite Monnot

THE POOR PEOPLE OF PARIS
(La Goualante du Pauvre Jean)

Songwriters have always loved "city songs." In the U.S. alone (not even considering New York and New Orleans), one can think of dozens: "St. Louis Blues," "Sioux City Sue," "Wichita Lineman," "Galveston," "Seattle," "San Francisco," "By the Time I Get to Phoenix," "Chattanooga Choo Choo" and "Kalamazoo," to name just a few. Internationally, no city has received the melodic attention accorded the City of Light: "I Love Paris," "The Last Time I Saw Paris," "April in Paris." This addition to the long list of Parisian salutes was written by Marguerite Monnot and was an instrumental success for Les Baxter. Jack Lawrence, whose many hits include "If I Didn't Care," "Beyond the Sea" and "All or Nothing at All," penned these lyrics — and very well, too. But perhaps Lawrence was thinking of the French word gens instead of Jean when he heard the original title, for he turned one poverty-stricken Frenchman into all of Paris's poor.

Old-time fox-trot tempo

The Poor People of Paris (La Goualante du Pauvre Jean)

peo – ple of Pa – ree.
Milk or *(repeat)*

peo – ple of Pa – ree.
So don't *(continue)*

go to Pa – ris, France, Not un – less you like to dance, Not un –

less you want ro – mance, Like those poor in – hab – i – tants of Pa –

ree.

ff

LILLI MARLENE
(My Lilli of the Lamplight)

English words by Tommie Connor; German words
by Hans Leip; Music by Norbert Schultze

*"Lilli Marlene" was one of the important songs of
World War II. It, of course, shares that distinction with
such novelty tunes as "Rosie the Riveter" and such
lovely nostalgic favorites as "The White Cliffs of
Dover." The difference is that "Lilli" was a favorite
with both German and Allied troops. The song's
international flavor was accentuated when Marlene
Dietrich adopted it as her own. Most people probably
look back upon even the most calamitous of times as
"the good old days," and no doubt some ex-soldier-
boy, now gray at the temples and somewhat long of
tooth, will smile wanly and take on a faraway look in
his eye as he plunks out this tune, thinking of the girl
"underneath the lantern by the barrack gate."*

Un – der-neath the lan – tern by the bar – rack gate,
Time would come for roll call, time for us to part;
Vor der Ka – ser – ne vor dem gros – sen Tor
Uns' – re bei – den Schat – ten sah'n wie ei – ner aus;

Dar – ling, I re-mem – ber the way you used to wait. 'Twas
Dar – ling, I'd ca-ress you and press you to my heart. And
Stand ei – ne La-ter – ne und steht sie noch da – vor,
Dass wir so lieb uns hat – ten sah man gleich da – raus.

* pronounced "Lily Marlane"

Orders came for sailing somewhere over there,
All confined to barracks was more than I could bear.
I knew you were waiting in the street;
I heard your feet but could not meet
My Lilli of the lamplight, my own Lilli Marlene.

Schon rief der Posten: sie blasen Zapfen seich;
Es kann drei Tage kosten! Kamerad ich komm' ja gleich.
Da sagten wir auf Wiedersehn.
Wie gerne wollt ich mit dir geh'n
Mit dir Lili Marleen, mit dir Lili Marleen.

Resting in a billet just behind the line,
Even though we're parted, your lips are close to mine.
You wait where that lantern softly gleams;
Your sweet face seems to haunt my dreams,
My Lilli of the lamplight, my own Lilli Marlene.

Deine Schritte kennt sie, deinen zieren Gang,
Alle Abend brennt sie mich vergass sie lang.
Und sollte mir ein Leid gescheh'n,
Wer wird bei der Laterne steh'n,
Mit dir Lili Marleen, mit dir Lili Marleen.

Aus dem stillen Raume, aus der Erde Grund
Hebt mich wie im Träume dein verliebter Mund.
Wenn sich die späten Nebel dreh'n,
Werd ich bei der Laterne steh'n,
Wie einst Lili Marleen, wie einst Lili Marleen.

A TREE IN THE MEADOW

Margaret Whiting had the big hit record of this bucolic tune, and, as is usually the case, there's a story behind it. She recorded it in 1948. The musicians' strike was on, so Capitol Records dispatched conductor-arranger Frank DeVol to Europe to cut the instrumental track that would eventually accompany her. "I knew nothing about it," Maggie recalls. "They called me

Words and Music by Billy Reid

Margaret Whiting

Slowly

pp-as though from far away

There's a

tree in the mead-ow
al - ways re-mem-ber

With a
The__

stream drift-ing by
love in your eye

And
The

carved up - on that
day you carved up -

tree I see
on that tree

"I
"I

love you till I die."

I will

love you till I die."

But

fur-ther on down lov-ers' lane

A

accel. - - - a little faster

to the studio and said that they were going to try something different, that I was going to sing to a track already cut. Today, of course, the custom is commonplace, but at that time it was a brand-new technique. They never told me that it was cut overseas. It was perfectly legal, but I guess they were afraid that I might balk. In my naïveté, I remember saying, 'What a coincidence; it's in my key!' " She forgot all about the recording until she was stopped on the street by a song plugger a couple of weeks later. He congratulated her on her smash. "With what?" she asked. " 'A Tree in the Meadow'," he replied. "Oh, if it were only that easy today," laments Margaret, who continues to be a smash in nightclubs and concert halls.

THE BANANA BOAT SONG

(Day-O)

Arranged and Adapted by Dan Fox

for the calypso and West Indian folk-song craze that became so popular in 1956 and 1957, with such hits as "Matilda, Matilda," "Jamaica Farewell," "Come Back, Liza" and "Brown Skin Girl." In fact, Harry Belafonte was second only to Elvis Presley as the most popular singer of the '50s. Soon after Belafonte's recording, Stan Freberg did a marvelously funny parody. Freberg's version involves an attempt to record the song and centers on a recalcitrant beatnik bongo player who can't stand the singer's yelling "Day-o" and forces him to sing the phrase more and more quietly. Eventually, the bongoist locks the singer out of the studio, so that he has to sing through a glass window. But not for long. He crashes back in and utters the memorable words, "I came in through the window."

"The Banana Boat Song," or "Day-O" as it may be more commonly known to most people, was introduced by a group called The Tarriers in late 1956 on a Glory recording. However, the song was made famous by Harry Belafonte, whose 1957 version on RCA Victor sold more than a million copies. That same year it was interpolated into a Columbia film, Calypso Heat Wave, which starred none other than singer Johnny Desmond. Belafonte was, of course, almost singlehandedly responsible

Moderate calypso tempo

Day - o, Day - o, *(sung without accompaniment)* Day be light and I wan-na go home.

Six han', sev-en han', Checker he come to eight han' bunch, check de bunch, Day be light and I wan-na go home.

Day - o, Day - o, Day be light and I wan-na go home.

Reader's Digest has published ten other music books: *Family Songbook,*
Treasury of Best Loved Songs, Family Songbook of Faith and Joy,
Festival of Popular Songs, Great Music's Greatest Hits,
The Merry Christmas Songbook, Popular Songs That Will Live Forever,
Country and Western Songbook, Unforgettable Musical Memories and *Children's Songbook.*
You can order them from Reader's Digest, Pleasantville, New York 10570.
(A few songs appear in more than one book,
but the musical arrangements are different.)

Reader's Digest Fund for the Blind is publisher of the Large-Type Edition of *Reader's Digest.* For
subscription information about this magazine, please contact Reader's Digest Fund for the Blind, Inc.,
Dept. 250, Pleasantville, N.Y. 10570.